# Breaking

DEMCO

# Breaking

## —— *the* ——

# Sound Barrier

*by Nathan Aaseng*

JULIAN Ⓜ MESSNER

# PHOTO ACKNOWLEDGMENTS

**Bell Aircraft Corporation:** the X-1 in flight; **Smithsonian Institution:** the Wright Brothers, Louis Blériot, Focke-Wulf 190, American Mustang, British Supermarine Spitfire, Robert Goddard, Wernher von Braun and German scientists, the Messerschmitt Komet, the Bachem BP 20 Natter, Geoffrey de Havilland, Sr., the X-1 being dropped from the belly of a B-29; **UPI/Bettmann:** Hanna Reitsch, the Swallow, Chuck Yeager.

Cover and text design by Mike Freeland.

Published by Julian Messner, a division of Simon & Schuster
Simon & Schuster Building, Rockefeller Center
1230 Avenue of the Americas, New York, New York 10020

JULIAN MESSNER and colophon are trademarks of
Simon & Schuster, Inc.
Manufactured in the United States of America.

Lib. ed. 10   9   8   7   6   5   4   3   2   1
paper ed. 10   9   8   7   6   5   4   3   2   1

Library of Congress Cataloging-in-Publication Data

Aaseng, Nathan.
    Breaking the sound barrier / by Nathan Aaseng.
        p.     cm.
    Includes bibliographical references and index.
    Summary: Chronicles the events leading up to the breaking of the sound barrier,
focusing on the test pilots who risked their lives to achieve supersonic flight.
    1. High-speed aeronautics—History—Juvenile literature.
    2. Supersonic planes—History—Juvenile literature.
    [1. Aeronautics—History.   2. Supersonic planes—History.   3. Airplanes—History.]
    I. Title.
    TL551.5.A28   1991
    626.132'305—dc20
                                                                    91-23693
                                                                         CIP
                                                                          AC

ISBN 0-671-74212-4 (LSB)
ISBN 0-671-74213-2 (pbk.)

# Contents

# 1
# *The "Wall" in the Sky*

Colonel Signa Gilkey strapped himself into the latest mechanical monster crafted by airplane design wizards. The United States Army, the service branch in charge of the air force at that time, had made plans to purchase some of these new P-38 Lightning fighter planes in the fall of 1940, and Gilkey's job was to find out if they were as good as advertised.

Gilkey was putting his life on the line, for no matter how carefully the plans were drawn up, there was still a lot of guesswork involved in producing new aircraft. Aircraft designers, like everyone else, learn from their mistakes. Frequently it was the pilots who paid for those mistakes, sometimes with their lives.

Yet flirting with danger was part of what made test piloting so attractive to adventurous types. Risky as Gilkey's assignment was, many pilots would have jumped at the chance to trade places with him. Explorers, knights, and even cowboys had faded from the modern world, but there was still a place for heroes in the sky. Like the top broncobusters of the old West, test pilots displayed an air of supreme self-confidence.

Guiding his P-38 Lightning down the runway, Gilkey soared high into the air. The new high-speed aircraft performed well as the pilot reached the peak of his climb. After getting comfortable with the feel of the plane, Gilkey decided to try out a power dive, a maneuver that was an essential part of any combat pilot's training. He pointed the nose of the P-38 down at a steep angle. Having already surpassed the speed of most airplanes, the Lightning continued to accelerate as it plunged toward the earth.

Almost immediately, Gilkey saw that luck was not riding with him that day. One of those dreaded unexpected glitches had burst upon him as the nose of the P-38 dropped further toward the ground. The controls were jamming so badly that Gilkey could hardly steer the craft!

Although he was a veteran pilot, Gilkey had never experienced anything like this before. Only with the greatest effort was the colonel able to wrench the plane out of its dive. That was the end of power-dive testing for that day. Gilkey had seen enough to know that something weird was going on and that he was lucky to have escaped the first time. There was no point in pushing his luck. Shaken by the experience, he cautiously landed the plane.

The report that he delivered was not exactly what the Army, nor the plane's manufacturer, Lockheed Aircraft Corporation, wanted to hear. Something was wrong with the P-38 Lightning. Lockheed assigned their own chief test pilot, Ralph Virden, to check out the mysterious situation.

If Virden was disturbed by the thought of flying into the air in a plane that an experienced pilot had been unable to control, he did not show it. Again, the P-38 handled well during the early tests. The only way Virden could find out what Gilkey had been talking about was to try a dive. The test pilot tried some safer dives at first without incident. Having learned nothing about the problem he was investigating, he then launched into a power dive.

The P-38 Lightning pitched violently downward as it accelerated. Something began battering the plane with the force of a small hurricane! The P-38 pitched wildly about, shuddering under the onslaught of unknown forces. Virden had gone too far into his dive to pull out as Gilkey had. The elevator, the mechanism attached to the tail that is supposed to regulate the angle of the plane's descent or ascent, did nothing. Virden never recovered control of his plane. It slammed into the ground, killing him instantly. Investigators sifting through the wreckage were aghast at what they discovered. The tail had been ripped off and the entire plane had been so badly crumpled prior to the crash that it reminded one observer of what happens when a terrier shakes a rat.

The findings cast an uneasy pall over the pilots and aircraft companies. What was this sinister, invisible force that could tear apart a structurally sound airplane? The astounding theories of Albert Einstein and other physicists that had come to light since the turn of the century had shown the universe to be inhabited by forces and objects almost beyond human imagination. Was there something equally bizarre out there waiting to shred any airplane that flew beyond a certain speed?

## "ANGEL WINGS"

With the self-confidence that buoys test pilots, Lockheed's Milo Burcham believed he could succeed where Ralph Virden had failed. During a high-speed dive, Burcham found what he was looking for. The controls locked up and he was bounced around the cockpit by severe buffeting (knocking back and forth). The nose of the plane plunged ever downward despite all his attempts to pull out of the dive!

Burcham, fortunately, was luckier than Virden. He managed to wrestle control of his plane before it hit the ground, and then he landed it safely. But he admitted that the experience had scared him half to death.

What was happening? The simplest answer was that the P-38 Lightning had been poorly designed. Many experts believed there had to be some defect in the tail structure that was causing the problem. Those who clung to that explanation, however, were jolted by the discovery that other airplanes were also being battered by the same forces. Not only American planes such as P-38s and P-47s, but also Great Britain's Supermarine Spitfires. All of them were high-speed aircraft, and all suddenly started to go haywire during high-speed dives.

By this time, Nazi Germany's stunning victories in World War II had plunged all matters of aircraft design into a state of urgency. With British pilots desperately fighting off wave after wave of German attack planes, there was no time to sort out leisurely the problem of high-speed instability. A shipment of American P-38 Lightnings was delivered to England in 1942 to bolster the British air defenses. Allied pilots quickly discovered they had as much to fear from their own planes as from the enemy. Within a few weeks of the arrival of the P-38s, one pilot was killed and two miraculously escaped death in noncombat dives.

One young Army pilot, unruffled by warnings of high-speed problems, revved his airplane up to its top speed of 400 miles per hour as he leveled off at 35,000 feet. From that height, he shot down in an exhilarating dive toward the ground. Almost instantly, his control stick froze. The pilot could not budge it in any direction. The plane bucked and rattled. He had no more mastery of his craft than if he were sitting on a falling rock! Outside the cockpit, the pilot thought he saw a strange white, swirling mist, and all other noises were drowned out by an unearthly roar. Just when ground observers were cringing in anticipation of a crash, the plane nosed up and arched into the air.

Upon landing, the pilot reported the strange sounds and sights of his harrowing ride. After viewing the miraculous recovery and studying the mangled wings of the aircraft, one veteran pilot had an answer. "What you saw were angel wings and the roaring was their harps!" he muttered. He could see no other explanation for the man's survival.

Morale among Allied pilots sank with each accident and near miss. An Allied pilot was already under terrible stress without having to worry about whether his airplane would kill him. The phrase "coffin or crackers" was the pilots' grim acknowledgment of their chances of surviving the war in good health. At one point during the war it was estimated that a pilot stood a 1-in-10 chance of finishing his stint without being killed or treated for emotional or mental breakdown.

Lieutenant Colonel Cass Hough, who was technical director of the United States Army Eighth Fighter Command, decided that the only way to erase pilots' jitters over flying these new suicide planes was to meet the problem head-on. Again showing the brazen confidence of the test pilot, the native of Michigan took off in a P-38 Lightning on September 29, 1942 over British skies. He was going up to see for himself what had spooked the pilots.

When he reached an altitude of 41,000 feet, he calmly

pointed the nose of his P-38 down at the ground, opened up to full throttle, and dared this mysterious force to do its worst. Convinced that he could handle whatever situation came up, he explained that the "purpose of the dive was to ease the minds of the P-38 pilots" in Great Britain, and "to obtain data."

Hough quickly found out for himself that the horror stories floating about were no exaggeration. His plane started shaking and bucking so badly he could barely keep a grip on the control stick. As his craft spun wildly through a free fall, the pilot screamed for all he was worth in an attempt to counter the tremendous pressure in his ears.

Determined to carry out his mission, Hough took his hands off the controls to jot down notes on the effects of this force at various altitudes. But after 15 seconds, his scientific interest in this phenomenon was overwhelmed by his predicament. The plane dropped to 30,000 feet, 25,000 feet, 20,000 feet, boring straight for the ground. The control column was dead and Hough could do nothing about it.

There is a point of peril at which self-confidence of the most brilliant ace begins to crack. At three miles above the earth, Hough realized he was out of answers. Unless some miracle occurred, he knew he was counting down his last seconds of life.

At 15,000 feet, the miracle happened! For no apparent reason, the controls started working again. Hough was able to pull the P-38 out of the dive into a wide arc. By 8,000 feet, his plane was flying level and back under control.

If Hough's purpose had been to ease the minds of the P-38 pilots about the safety of their planes, he had failed badly. It seemed apparent that some mysterious force hovered in the sky, waiting to ambush high-speed aircraft.

Many aviation engineers were caught off guard by the experience and groped for an explanation. But at least one man had seen it coming. Back in 1937, Lockheed engineer Clarence "Kelly" Johnson had written a memo concerning the effects of high speed on aircraft. Johnson pointed out that the P-38 models were designed to fly so fast that the air flow passing over some portions of the plane would approach the speed of sound. Just what effect this unusual situation would have on a plane was anybody's guess. But Johnson predicted that this situation would begin to occur when an airplane reached a speed near two-thirds the speed of sound. At high altitudes, the speed of sound was just under 700 miles per hour. Two-thirds of that was about 465 miles per hour. That was approximately the speed at which a power-diving fighter plane stopped acting like an airplane and began resembling a falling meteor.

## THE "SOUND BARRIER"

Johnson's analysis turned out to be correct. When an object approaches the speed of sound, the normal laws of aviation no longer apply. The air around it does not act as it normally would. In 1935 British aircraft designer Dr. W. F. Hilton of the National Physical Labs, while explaining some wind-tunnel data to a newsman said, "See how the resistance of a wing shoots up like a barrier against higher speeds as we approach the speed of sound."

The term "sound barrier" gave reporters a vivid image of what was happening in aviation research. The description caught on. Before the end of World War II, even the general public was familiar with the expression.

The word "barrier" has been commonly used since then to describe milestones in achievement. For example, in

1954 Roger Bannister of Great Britain was the first to crack the widely acclaimed "four-minute barrier" in running the mile. The term has also been used to describe psychological barriers, such as those restricting women and minorities from full participation in society.

From the safe perspective of hindsight, some may scorn the sound barrier as a scarecrow or a bogeyman—a superstitious fear of the unknown that modern technology has easily blown away. But the sound barrier was not just a milestone, nor merely a goal for engineers to shoot for. The pilots caught in the death spin of a suddenly berserk P-38 Lightning could testify that it was no figment of the imagination. To the aviation world in the 1940s, the barrier was as real as a wall in the sky. Something strange was happening at near sonic speeds; and whatever it was, it was killing pilots.

Sound travels at different speeds depending on the temperature of the air. At higher elevations, the air temperature is colder. Therefore, the speed of sound is around 760 miles per hour at sea level at a temperature of 75 degrees Fahrenheit, then tails off to 662 miles per hour above 35,000 feet. Many experts suspected that if an airplane were able to fly at those speeds, it would blow up the instant it hit that magic sonic number. That was all sheer speculation, though, because many believed that long before a plane reached that speed, the sonic forces would slam and twist it into a piece of junk.

Others believed there had to be some way to get past the mysterious sound barrier. After all, it was certainly not impossible for objects to exceed the speed of sound. Rockets had been fired at speeds of nearly five times the speed of sound. All that was needed was to determine exactly what happens to the air around a plane as it approaches the speed of sound, and then make adjustments.

In the 1940s, no one knew for certain what the sound barrier was. Was it a permanent, unyielding force? Or was it just another in a series of problems to be overcome? Dr. Theodore von Kármán, director of the Guggenheim Aeronautical Laboratory at the California Institute of Technology, one of the most respected figures in American aviation industry, summed up the situation in the early 1940s. When asked whether it was possible to fly at the speed of sound, he replied, "I do not believe that at the present time, the answer can be yes or no."

Neither fear nor uncertainty prevented the world's most skilled pilots from looking for the answer. The rash of power-dive fatalities did not scare aviation researchers away from high-speed testing. Many more daring pilots volunteered to try power dives and other maneuvers in order to gain information that might help other pilots. A British pilot named W. K. Stewart actually blacked out more than 200 times while performing test flights measuring the effects of acceleration.

It was a test pilot's job to walk on the edge of danger. Like the pioneers who scouted out the hidden passes through intimidating mountain ranges, these men and women eventually discovered the paths that led to supersonic speed.

# 2
# Speed in the Air

For those who have grown up in the space age, it is accepted without question that the vehicles best equipped for speed are those that travel through the air, freed from the friction of contact with the ground. Yet in the early days of the airplane that was still a debatable point. The plane that the Wright brothers first lifted off the ground near Kitty Hawk, North Carolina, on December 17, 1903, took 59 seconds to travel 852 feet. This would mean that the Wright's machine puttered through the air at less than 7 miles per hour. It would have taken a giant leap of imagination for someone to predict that an airplane could someday fly at the speed of sound.

These underpowered flying contraptions were viewed more as amusement-park rides. Many of the early planes were so sluggish that they could actually be blown backward by a stiff wind. Yes, it was wonderful that the Wrights had realized the ancient dream of human flight. However, there was no practical use for an airplane; it could not compete with the speed of a land-based vehicle, such as a train. Trains were not only faster but safer, more convenient, and could carry far more passengers and freight than a flying machine. If they were ever to find a useful niche in the world, airplanes would have to be able to fly faster.

Operational speed in any sort of mechanized transportation depends on two things: 1) how fast the object can be made to travel and 2) how well the object can be controlled at that speed. The evolution of aircraft from slow, fluttering hobby toys into supersonic engineering marvels has been a continuous game of leapfrog getting the plane to go faster and finding a way to control that speed.

First, small engines, light enough to propel a flimsy frame into the air, were developed in the late 1800s. This proved worthless as far as air travel because no one knew how to control a flying vehicle. Then Wilbur and Orville Wright developed their wing-warping system of control. Using a series of cables attached to the front and rear edges of the wings, the Wrights were able to adjust the angle of the wings so that a flying craft could be controlled under a variety of conditions.

Once the Wrights achieved control over their slow-moving aircraft, the speed of aircraft was then limited by the power of the engines and by the drag (the pull on the aircraft in the opposite direction). The Wrights and other inventors sought out more powerful engines that could fly their planes up to speeds of about 30 miles per hour.

That seemed to be the limit that could be achieved with the standard engines and aircraft designs of the time. Larger engines could be built but would be too heavy to be practical. Faster-running engines could be built, but there was no way to keep them from overheating.

In 1909 two French brothers and engineers, Louis and Laurent Seguin, designed a revolutionary new engine. This was the rotary engine, in which the entire body of the engine spun along with the propellors. The revolving engine was able to improve the airflow over the cylinders, and so solved the cooling problem that had thwarted most designers. The Seguins and other French airplane enthusiasts quickly elevated their country to the forefront of aviation technology. As early as 1908, French planes were said to have achieved 40 miles per hour.

# RACING IN THE AIR

Since airplanes were still considered a frivolous novelty, almost all of the flying and designing was done by amateurs. Aviation buffs joined together to form clubs in which they could pool their knowledge and resources to promote their hobby. They began to set up races and keep records of who could fly the fastest, the longest, and the highest.

At first these activities were carried out on a small, haphazard scale, much like Frisbee competitions today. The first recorded speed record for an airplane was credited to a Brazilian living in Paris, Alberto Santos-Dumont. On November 12, 1906, Santos-Dumont was clocked at 25.65 miles per hour in his awkward, unstable, kite-like biplane.

As time went on, others claimed to have flown faster. In order to insure accuracy in air records, race standards were set up by the Fédération Aéronautique Internationale. The first to qualify under this sanction was Paul Tissandier, a student at Wilbur Wright's aviation school in Pau, France. Tissandier, the first European to stay in the air over an hour, was officially timed at 34.04 miles per hour on May 20, 1909.

By the summer of that year, aviation clubs began to think on a grander scale. An international week of demonstrations and competition was set up in late August at Reims, France. Airplane pilots were invited to bring their craft to demonstrate their skill. One of the many entrants was an American inventor named Glenn Curtiss. Late in the week, Curtiss stunned the French by reaching a top average speed of 43.35 miles per hour. One of the men he defeated, Louis Blériot, reclaimed the record for France before the week was out with a best effort of 47.85 miles per hour.

The quest for speed gained momentum. The French introduced new, streamlined aircraft designs that cut down on the amount of drag and wind resistance. This, plus continued improvements in engine design enabled pilots to approach the mile-per-minute mark.

But with the latest increase in speed, the pendulum swung back to the other side—to the problem of learning to control that speed. While many of an airplane's handling characteristics could be determined in wind tunnels and other laboratory conditions, much of the experimentation could only be done in actual flight by test pilots.

## EARLY TEST PILOTS

The world's first test pilots displayed the cool, death-defying confidence that has since become their trademark. British test pilot Wilfred Parke set the standard with an advertisement he placed in the May 1911 issue of *Flight* magazine: "Why break your Aeroplane yourself . . . when we can do it for you?" Parke's ad was directed to British designers who were building their own flying machines.

Parke was one of the first test pilots to recognize the need for finding the airplane's limits of safety. Airplane builders needed to determine the top speed at which a plane could be flown safely as well as the ability of the airplane's structure to stand up to the stress of various maneuvers. Parke also recognized that the only way you could find those limits was to push a plane to the edge of those limits. The 22-year-old Parke was the first person to put an airplane into a spin intentionally in order to see how well the plane could correct the problem. He wrote the first handbook for test pilots, in which he described what tests were most useful in determining an airplane's abilities.

Parke also led the procession of test pilots into an early grave. In 1912 the young daredevil tested an airplane to see how well it responded to a stalled engine during flight. Unfortunately, he found out the answer. Parke failed to recover from the stall and crashed to his death.

French test pilots, meanwhile, pushed the limits of speed far beyond their rivals. On July 10, 1910, Leon Morane passed the mile-per-minute milestone with a record speed of 66.19. Jules Védrines established another memorable first for the French by flying an airplane more than 100 miles per hour on February 2, 1912.

French innovation in engine and airplane body design kept them well ahead of the rest of the world for more than a decade. Thirty new airplane speed records were set from 1909 to 1922—every one of them achieved by a French pilot! The price of this speed, however, was as expensive for the French as it was for everyone else. Several years after setting his speed record, Jules Védrines stepped over the limit of safety one time too often, and died in a crash.

Heading into World War I, most airplanes still held no speed advantage over land-based methods of transportation. At the beginning of the war, inventor Glenn Curtiss could travel faster on a motorcycle than he could in his fastest airplane. But by the beginning of the 1920s, the airplane was beginning to pull away as the world's fastest vehicle. Improvements in aircraft structure design made it possible for faster, more streamlined monoplanes—planes with a single wing—to compete with the double-decker biplanes. Wood propellors were beginning to be replaced by stronger, thinner metal blades that were able to spin faster and withstand greater stress.

## SEAPLANE RACES

Following a break during the war, aviation clubs continued their pursuit of speed. Much of their activity was centered on seaplanes. The most famous races were for the Schneider Trophy, which was begun in 1913. From the mid-1920s through the 1930s, most world-speed records were set by seaplanes designed for this amateur competition. Aviation experts took the Schneider Trophy seriously. After several years of embarrassing performances in Schneider Trophy races, the British responded by enlisting the Royal Air Force (RAF) in 1918 to improve their capabilities.

Schneider Trophy races, unfortunately, often generated more controversy than genuine competition. In 1919, for example, the race was held near Bournemouth along the English coast. A circular two-mile course was set up and marked by boats anchored at various positions in the water. Race organizers scheduled the 10-lap 20-mile race for 2 o'clock in the afternoon.

The weather did not cooperate, and the problems caused by a heavy mist were compounded by indecisive race organizers. The starting time was moved back to 6 p.m., then pushed forward to 4:30. The announcement of yet another change, back to 4:45, was too much for the exasperated French team, and they refused to take part.

The British contestants were eager to take advantage of the absence of the favored French. Three of them took to the foggy skies on their first lap of the 10-lap race. Visibility was so poor, though, that two of the three quit after one lap. The third had to land in the bay to figure out his location. While taking off from there, the plane sustained such damage that it sank upon landing again at Bournemouth.

That left the Italian entry in control of the race. Despite the miserable conditions, the Italian posted tremendous lap times as he buzzed around the course. In fact, his times were impossibly fast. Race officials sent him around for one more lap in case someone had counted wrong. While doing so, the Italian ran out of fuel and had to make an emergency landing. It was then discovered that, confused by the mist, he had been flying around a reserve marker boat that was docked near the shore instead of the real one. The Italian was disqualified, the whole race was declared void, and nearly everyone went away angry.

While not all Schneider Cup races turned into such a fiasco, this particular race was a foreshadowing of the fate of the amateur airplane club. The field of aviation had grown out of its infancy. It was quickly growing too large, complex, and expensive to be handled by weekend tinkerers.

This was as true for airplane-speed records as it was for race organization. Airplanes began to travel so fast that they made a mockery of the official rules for setting speed records. According to the international federation's rules, an airplane had to reach its speed at a level height of less than 75 meters (246 feet) above the ground. It could not rise above 400 meters (1,312 feet) while making a turn. Those height limitations, while reasonable for planes traveling at

100 miles per hour, became ever more dangerous as aircraft speeds increased.

Also, whereas new speed records could once be achieved by airplane hobbyists who dabbled with the basic engine or design of the wings, the latest innovations in technology were starting to go beyond the means of most individuals. New materials, such as strong, lightweight metals and innovative types of engines, required enormous research and development efforts. This type of effort could be carried out only by corporations that had the money and research staff to explore the new possibilities.

The amateur racing clubs did not lose their dominance all at once. It took nearly two decades for them to fade from the scene. During that time, seaplane races nudged the speed records well into the 300 mile-per-hour range. Each new record was primarily the result of larger and more powerful gasoline engines. Again, every increase in engine power required a brave test pilot to prove that this power could be controlled. Dozens of pilots were killed by these powerful new machines in testing and during races in the 1920s and early 1930s.

## FROM FRIENDLY COMPETITION TO GRIM STRUGGLE

While the Schneider Trophy seaplanes continued to bask in the glory of new records, corporations were quietly taking over the field of aviation. Their large financial resources were further strengthened by aid from governments who recognized the importance of airplanes in warfare and saw aviation technology as crucial to their defense.

In the late 1930s, the combined might of government and industry overwhelmed the romantic speed dreams of the amateur-airplane buffs. A fierce duel for air supremacy being two giants of the German aircraft industry spelled the end for amateur-speed champions. Following Hitler's rise to power in 1933, Germany poured an enormous amount of energy into their military. Ernst Heinkel and Willy Messerschmitt were two influential aircraft designers who were charged with the mission of building up Nazi Germany's air power. At the same time, both coveted the honor of creating the world's fastest airplanes.

Heinkel's chances of claiming this honor were sabotaged by the German aviation authorities. They awarded government contracts for swift-flying fighter planes to Messerschmitt, and left Heinkel to build the less glamorous, slower-flying bombers. Bitter at what he felt was a snub to his engineering reputation, Heinkel set out to break the world-speed record. His He 100 was not designed as a practical fighter plane. It was built strictly for the purpose of putting Ernst Heinkel in the record books as the world's airspeed champion. On March 30, 1939, an He 100 roared through the air at an average speed of 463.9 miles per hour, shattering the former mark.

Heinkel's victory, however, was short-lived. Messerschmitt was equally determined to claim the top spot for himself. Using every last refinement of conventional aircraft design and construction, he built his own experimental aircraft, the Me 209, whose only purpose was to top Heinkel's effort. The undersized plane was packed with such a maximum of power and a minimum of grace and control that its pilot, Luftwaffe officer Fritz Wendel, described it as "a vicious little brute." On April 26, 1939, less than a month after Heinkel claimed the record, Wendel streaked through the skies over Germany at an average speed of 469.2.

At that point, the age of trophies and races was over. The amateur clubs and shade-tree mechanics had reshaped airplanes from slow, puttering, modified kites into streamlined racers. They had boosted the speed at which humans could travel to about half the speed of sound. Any further improvements would come from corporate investment, research organizations, and government tax dollars.

Before 1939 was over, the airplanes of Heinkel, Messerschmitt, and every other aircraft manufacturer in the world were engaged in a competition far more deadly than claiming a speed record. Germany lauched a massive attack on Poland that touched off the most terrible, widespread war ever fought. Much of the credit for the German's swift conquest of Poland went to the effectiveness of their air force. Suddenly the airplane became essential to a nation's survival.

Military leaders in many Western countries began to give top priority to designing airplanes that were stronger and faster, more efficient and more maneuverable. Careful not to give away any possible advantage to the enemy, their test flights were held in secret. When speed records were broken, they were not announced. Nor were any technological advances made public. Airplanes were getting faster, but few people had an accurate picture as to which was the fastest. The quest for speed had degenerated from a friendly competition between sportsmen to a grim struggle between nations.

At one time or another during World War II, the German Focke-Wulf 190, the British Supermarine Spitfire, and the American P-51 Mustang, P-38 Lightning, and P-47 Thunderbolt was each heralded as the world's fastest airplane. There were reports in the media of pilots pushing these conventional, propeller-driven aircraft into power dives reaching speeds in excess of 600 miles per hour. Some pilots claimed to have topped 800 miles per hour, which if true, would have carried them past the speed of sound.

As a matter of fact, the propeller-driven fighter aircraft of World War II could improve little upon the 460-mile-per-hour speeds of the Heinkel and Messerschmitt experimentals. This was not surprising to most aircraft engineers. An airplane propeller could provide only so much thrust (forward motion), and aircraft designers believed they were already straining at the limits of what a propeller could accomplish. Setting aside for a moment the problems of control and the shock waves that pilots were beginning to experience at the highest speeds of propeller-driven planes, some new method of thrust would have to be found if airplanes were to travel significantly faster.

It was time for another phase in the assault on speed records—a search for new methods of power. The jet engine and the rocket engine would someday push humankind to the edge of the sound barrier. But in the early stages, these were raw, unmanagable powers. They were liable to explode at any moment or to instantly pitch the most skilled pilot into a death spin. Taming this power would be a crucial challenge.

# 3
# Supersonic Power—
# Jets and Rockets

## JETS

In 1941 an official report written for the United States government wrote off the possible development of the jet engine as impractical. According to the research and calculations cited in the report, the most efficient jet engine would weigh 13 times the amount of thrust it could produce. There was not much point in trying to fly under those conditions.

Had it been made available, these conclusions would have provided hilarious reading for German engineers. Nearly two years *before*, a German pilot had already successfully flown a jet plane!

Jet engines were not a new idea that suddenly surfaced around the time of World War II. Romanian inventors had been experimenting with the concept back in the days when the Wright brothers were perfecting their flying machines. Henri Coanda of Romania actually built a prototype jet airplane in 1910, although it did not fly successfully enough to attract further interest.

What is a jet engine? Jet engines are basically devices that produce a forward movement by shooting a steady, powerful flow of gases toward the rear of the vehicle. Like a conventional engine, this requires a continuous burning of a high-energy fuel. But it also calls for a high volume of air that must be compressed so that it is under great pressure. The mechanical motion in a jet engine is supplied by a turbine that is caused to spin by the pressurized air.

The idea of jet propulsion was so intriguing that aviation engineers kept returning to it over the years, hoping it could somehow be made to work. In the 1920s, a considerable amount of exploration went into jet engines. As before, the problems seemed insurmountable. One engineer who did not give up was Frank Whittle of Great Britain.

In 1923 Whittle, a 16-year-old apprentice studying at the Royal Air Force College, began experimenting with jet propulsion. One of the main problems he encountered was that the blistering heat produced by the gas-turbine jet quickly destroyed the engine. Eventually, new heat-resistant materials were created that could stand up to the stress, allowing Whittle to succeed in developing a practical gas-turbine engine. He applied for his first patents on his invention in 1930, and received approval in 1932. A generous man and loyal to his country, Whittle refused to exercise any rights on his patents while serving with the Royal Air Force, and let the patent expire in 1935. The jet engine was basically his gift to his country.

While Whittle gave Great Britain a head start, it did not take long for a rival nation to catch up. Germany's Hans von Ohain developed his own jet engine in the mid-1930s, while working for Heinkel. From there, German engineers proceeded much more quickly than did their British counter-parts. Stung by Germany's defeat in World War I, Adolf Hitler's government was constantly looking for ways to gain a military advantage. It was common knowledge that at about half the speed of sound and at altitudes above 25,000 feet, propellers became less efficient at providing power. Propeller-driven planes were approaching their limits, and there was little room for any innovation in internal-combustion engines that would give their air force a decisive advantage. A jet engine, on the other hand, had the potential to provide enormous power, assuming that certain problems were overcome.

Working to overcome those difficulties, engineers installed a jet engine in a Heinkel fighter plane. German pilots who were assigned to fly the craft were suspicious of this new power plant. The pilots wanted to know how much horsepower the engine could put out, but the output of a jet engine was measured in pounds not in horsepower.

Despite these doubts, on August 27, 1939, Erich War-sitz took off in his experimental He 178 from a runway at Marienke, Germany. Six minutes later, he brought the plane in for a landing for the first successful jet-powered flight in history.

The jet project was then transferred to Messerschmitt, who was responsible for building the bulk of the German fighter planes. Production began in late 1941. By this time enough of the problems had been smoothed over so that test pilots were excited about taking the jet into the air. One pilot commented that when he took off in the Me 262 jet fighter, "It was as though angels were pushing me."

While Messerschmitt was designing and testing the Me 262, Great Britain was scrambling to recapture the lead they had squandered in jet-aircraft technology. Not until 1941, two years after Germany's first jet flight, did Great Britain's first test jet plane take off into the skies. The British quickly narrowed the gap, however. By the time Germany's Me 262 roared into combat in 1944, Britain's Gloster Meteor jets were ready for action. Both versions of the jet could easily outrun the fastest propeller fighters. Initially, the Me 262 was judged the faster of the two. It could reach speeds in level flight of around 525 miles per hour. By the end of the war, the Gloster Meteors were pushing 550 miles per hour. The wartime development of jet aircraft meant that humans were suddenly 100 miles per hour closer to the speed of sound.

## ROCKETS

If the United States was backward in its evaluation and pursuit of jet aircraft, its negligence in recognizing the potential of rocket power was even more embarrassing. After all, the world's foremost rocket pioneer was an American, a Massachusetts college professor named Robert Goddard. Goddard, who was obsessed by the idea of space flight, received patents for rocket-engine work as early as 1914. Working in his spare time, using his own money supplemented by a small grant from the Smithsonian Institution, Goddard launched the world's first liquid-propellant rocket on March 16, 1926.

Goddard devoted his entire life to rocket technology and eventually claimed more than 200 patents. To this day virtually every rocket launched employs inventions and systems that Goddard patented, yet his remarkable efforts drew mostly scorn from his fellow Americans. His theories were ridiculed in newspaper editorials and brushed aside by United States military authorities.

While Goddard shielded himself from criticism by retreating into his own secret, one-man operation, his ideas were finding a much more favorable audience across the ocean. German scientists saw clearly that Goddard was onto something. In 1927 Professor Hermann Oberth wrote a scholarly paper describing the capabilities of liquid-fuel rockets. Rather than chuckling up their sleeves at Oberth and Goddard, German engineers and inventors took them at their word and raced to see who could harness this wonderful power first. The limiting factor with rocket engines was that they provided power in short, uncontrollable explosions. German engineers probed for ways to tame these bursts so that a longer, reasonably comfortable ride could be achieved. Various designs for rocket-powered automobiles and airplanes were drawn up. In 1928 one experimenter solved the problem by attaching a series of 24 rockets to a car. The system was designed so that the rockets went off in a relay, one after another. This relay system boosted the car to a top speed of 137 miles per hour. Later that year other engineers managed to launch a glider plane with a rocket engine into the air.

It was an automobile manufacturer who led the way in rocket-engine research. Fritz von Opel's motives were not scientific at all. His main goal in financing rocket experiments was to gain free publicity for his company. Opel's cars would gain considerable prestige if he could connect them in the public's mind to superpowered rockets.

Opel not only provided the financing and the mechanical skill, he even did the actual testing. On September 30, 1928, he took off in his own rocket-propelled glider near Frankfurt. He sailed nearly 5,000 feet, reaching a top speed of 95 miles per hour. From this promising start, the project rapidly deteriorated. Opel did not feel bound by the test pilots' bravado. As later test flights began crashing well short of their goals, he decided not to push his luck. Satisfied with the publicity he had received and feeling fortunate not to have lost any lives in the process, Opel brought his experiments to an end.

There were plenty, however, who were eager to pick up where Opel had left off. Many of them, though, were not as lucky. Gottlob Espenlaub succeeded in piloting a rocket-powered modified glider in May of 1930. But in a later test, one of his rockets failed to work during takeoff. Espenlaub was able to get airborne without the rocket; but while in the air, the pilot accidentally ignited the rocket. This shot Espenlaub's plane straight into the ground. The inventor was lucky to survive the incident.

The tremendous power that made rockets so appealing made experimentation with them hazardous to on-ground researchers as well as pilots. One of Germany's leading rocket engineers, Max Valier, provided a grim reminder of this while tinkering with an experimental motor on May 17, 1930. The engine blew up, and Valier was killed. Later experiments with Hellmuth Walter's new hydrogen peroxide fuel blew up entire buildings. Accidents such as these dampened some of the enthusiasm among the world's engineers for working with rockets. Much of the private rocket research in the early 1930s focused on unmanned rockets.

But no matter how dangerous the experiments, rocket power remained a tempting research target for those determined to exploit every possible military advantage. As part of Adolf Hitler's massive rearming of Germany in the 1930s, a huge, secret effort was made to harness the power of liquid fuel rockets as a means of helping overloaded aircraft to take off. Eventually, there was talk of building a high-speed rocket fighter plane.

In 1936 a young scientist named Wernher von Braun pushed forward with a program to equip fighter planes with liquid fuel rockets. The fuels were extremely volatile, and no one yet knew how to design a safe way of handling them. But after von Braun demonstrated how, Ernst Heinkel agreed to provide him with He 112 fighters for experiments. Because of the risk, initial tests of the rocket plane were run by remote control. The caution proved to be well-founded. The first two rocket-equipped Heinkels exploded.

## "KICKED IN THE BACKSIDE"

By March 1937, however, von Braun thought that the project had advanced enough to try piloted flight. A courageous test pilot named Erich Warsitz was recruited to make the historic trip from an empty emergency landing strip outside of Berlin. Although a conventional piston engine would provide backup power in case the rocket engine did not work, that could not have been of much comfort to Warsitz. He had to wedge himself into a cockpit surrounded by liquid oxygen and alcohol tanks that could blow up without warning.

Warsitz started up the piston engine. With the plane still standing on the runway, he then carefully followed instructions to prepare the rocket motor for ignition. Everything was going smoothly until he eased forward the lever to fire the rocket. Instantly an explosion shattered the plane! The engine was thrown in one direction, Warsitz flew off in another, and pieces of aircraft sailed everywhere.

Somehow, Warsitz crawled away from the disaster with

only a few bumps and cuts. True to the test-pilot's spirit, he was undaunted by his narrow escape. Immediately he went to Heinkel to express his confidence in the program and to persuade him to contribute more planes to the effort. One month later, Warsitz was back on the same airfield ready to try again.

This time Warsitz took off using the piston engine. When he reached a height of 2,600 feet and a speed of about 190 miles per hour, he reached for the rocket-ignition lever. The airplane shot forward to 250 miles per hour, then continued to accelerate as it climbed into the air, spewing flame in its wake. Warsitz felt as though he had been "kicked in the backside." After thirty seconds, the rocket fuel was exhausted and Warsitz landed safely. In June of 1937, Warsitz took off using only the power of his rocket engine, and completed the world's first controlled rocket-powered flight.

Heinkel, who was in the midst of his campaign to win the world-speed record, saw the rocket as the means to assure his superiority. Working on his own without government backing, he began constructing the He 176, the first experimental airplane powered solely by rocket engines. He made the plane as small as possible so that the engines had less to push. The cockpit was custom-built to Erich Warsitz's dimensions, and he was squeezed into it like a hand into a glove.

In this cramped condition, Warsitz continued to flirt with death during tests of this plane. The rocket engine was still an all-or-nothing affair: if it kicked in at all, it kicked in at full power. These sudden lurches guaranteed that there was no such thing as a routine ignition. The He 176 also had such trouble getting off the ground that its small wings had to be redesigned. It was not until June 20, 1939, that Warsitz got an He 176 to lumber off the runway for a 50-second flight.

Just when the He 176 began making real progress, German air ministers abandoned it because this odd-looking, tiny craft had no immediate military purpose, and Germany was on the verge of war. For all his daring in pioneering the rocket-engine plane, Erich Warsitz would never get a chance to take it up to challenge the dragons of speed.

The Messerschmitt company, meanwhile, had a rocket-fighter program of its own. The government's disdain for rocket fighters meant that Messerschmitt was allowed to work on it only when there was extra time, for example, while waiting for a shipment of materials or parts for their regular fighters. But when Heini Dittmar regularly began topping 300 miles per hour in an experimental craft and showing spectacular climb rates, the German authorities changed their minds. Beginning in 1940, the Me 163, as the Messerschmitt rocket-plane fighter was designated, became a high priority.

The experienced Dittmar was again called upon to break in the new operational model of the Me 163 at Germany's new secret experimental center at Peenemünde, near the Baltic Sea. He barely survived the early nonpowered glider trials that were done to see how well the plane handled. On at least two occasions, Dittmar ran out of landing space before he could bring the plane down.

By July of 1941, enough of the problems had been worked out so that Dittmar was ready for full test flights. These went smoothly. Unknown to the rest of the world, Dittmar began regularly shattering the existing speed records. While still familiarizing himself with the plane, Dittmar raced through the sky at 550 miles per hour.

On October 2, 1941, Dittmar was towed in his Me 163A into the sky behind a fighter plane. At 13,120 feet, the towline was released and the rocket plane dropped away and began gliding. Dittmar immediately ignited his rocket engines and blazed through the sky. He had reached the incredible speed of 624 miles per hour and was still accelerating when the mysterious force in the sky bore down on him. The Me 163A started buffeting and then pitched nose down into a dive. Wisely, Dittmar shut off the rocket motor. The craft slowed down quickly and the pilot was able to regain control.

At first the German authorities refused to believe that the Me 163A had flown that fast. But the results were confirmed. Dittmar had flown at more than 80 percent of the speed of sound and had lived to tell about it. The bizarre loss of control that Dittmar had experienced at high speed was as much a concern to German engineers as to their American and British counterparts. The Germans set out to redesign the shape of the wings and aircraft body to try to minimize those effects.

## "THE DEVIL'S BROOMSTICK"

While these changes were being planned, another country leapfrogged over the Germans to the forefront of rocket-plane technology. Unknown to most of the world, it was the Soviet Union that developed the first successful, genuine rocket-propelled fighter plane. Dittmar's Me 163A was not a fighter plane but rather an unarmed experimental model designed to test some of the proposed aviation advances. Nearly a year before Germany trotted out their finished version of the Me 163 Komet fighter, the Soviets' 21-foot long BI interceptor had been ready for action.

The man who tamed this little monster of the skies in the early months of 1942 was Grigori Bakhchivandzhe. Bakhchivandzhe started collecting his test-flight battle scars early. During a ground test of the first BI, he accidentally opened the throttle too quickly. The resulting explosion burned three test assistants and sent Bakhchivandzhe to the hospital with a severe concussion.

But by May, Bakhchivandzhe was back in action. During a runway test he nudged the plane off the ground for a few moments and was satisfied that the plane handled well. On May 15, under cloudy skies, Bakhchivandzhe fired up the engines and zoomed down the runway. Airborne within 60 yards, he climbed steeply to 2,600 feet. Although the landing was rough, the three-minute flight was a success, and the Soviets now held the advantage in the race for speed. Confident of success, they prepared a fleet of BIs for production.

The Soviets ran half a dozen test flights of the BI, each time turning the engines up a notch and gaining greater speed. The awesome experience of blasting into the air on a tail of fire prompted one pilot to report that the craft "flew like the devil's broomstick."

According to engineering calculations, the armed BI was capable of flying over 600 miles per hour. On March 27, 1943, Bakhchivandzhe took off to see how close to that speed he could come. Streaking along at 6,560 feet, the pilot accelerated to a speed estimated somewhere around 500 miles per hour.

But he had wandered too close to the forbidden zone and Bakhchivandzhe's plane fell into that characteristic nose-down pitch. As it plunged and spun toward the earth, the unseen forces tore apart the BI as they had the American and British fighters. Bakhchivandzhe's first experience with the dreaded "sonic barrier" would be his last. He never came close to recovering control and slammed into the ground.

Soviet aviation experts then conducted wind-tunnel tests which showed the puzzling tendency of the plane to pitch downward at high speeds. Unsure of how to overcome the problem, they scuttled the entire Soviet rocket fighter program. There was no sense in building speed into aircraft if that speed could not be controlled.

## TEST-PILOT TRAGEDY

With the Soviets out of the airspeed picture before anyone knew they were in, the Germans had the field entirely to themselves. The next step for them was to build a practical rocket fighter that could be used in the war. As 1942 progressed, there was so much test work to be performed on the new Me 163B models that Heini Dittmar was joined by veteran test pilot Rudolf Opitz.

Late in 1942, Dittmar was testing an improved landing flap design when he made a serious error. (The landing flap is the extension of the trailing edge of the wing that creates greater lift.) The test pilot who had flown faster than any other person alive suffered his worst accident while slowly gliding only 12 feet off the ground. Coasting in for a landing next to the hangar, he accidentally encountered a windless space behind the hangar. The plane stalled and dropped like an anvil. The pilot's spinal cord was so badly damaged in the crash that Dittmar had to spend the next two years in a hospital. The quest for speed had claimed yet another victim.

In July of 1943, Opitz began to test-fly the rocket-powered Me 163B Komet. The Komet did not have regular landing wheels; instead, it took off supported by a dolly that was jettisoned as the plane became airborne and landed on skids (that look something like skis). In Opitz's initial run, the dolly detached before his plane reached takeoff speed. Given the explosive nature of the fuel filling his tanks, Opitz faced a fiery death if he could not get the plane off the ground. He barely managed to lift the plane up but then faced a new problem. Steam from the fuel tanks began shooting into the cockpit, nearly blinding him. The pilot was able to eject the canopy of the cockpit before he was consumed by the steam then landed safely despite the fact that he could barely see.

Opitz's luck ran out when his landing gear jammed several weeks later. Forced to land without it, he was so jolted upon hitting the ground that he suffered spinal injuries remarkably similar to Dittmar's, and spent three months in the hospital.

Dittmar and Opitz proved to be some of the more fortunate test pilots, for the flaming rocket planes took a heavy toll on the Germans. On December 30, 1943, Joseph Pohs made what appeared to be a successful takeoff. The steel dolly separated as the plane started to rise, just as it was supposed to, but it rebounded so hard off the ground that it struck the aircraft. Although Pohs was able to keep the Komet steady, the collision ruptured a fuel line. After climbing sharply for a short way, the plane crashed, killing the pilot.

During the first powered takeoffs of the Me 163B Komet in 1943, Alois Worndl was selected to make the initial run. Some of the German rocket plane trials had been moved to an airfield farther inland, near Bad Zwischenahn, to get away from the intense Allied bombing raids. Worndl took off from this airfield and piloted his craft skillfully to a height of nearly 20,000 feet before running out of rocket fuel.

Gliding in for a landing, Worndl was unable to bring the plane down at the proper angle, and overshot the landing field. His plane hit the ground, bounced into the air, crashed and flipped onto its back, engulfed in flames.

## HANNA REITSCH

But the most famous of all the pilots to wrestle with the controls of the deadly Komet was Hanna Reitsch. The daughter of an eye specialist, Reitsch had decided at an early age that she would be a flying missionary doctor. While her parents approved of both her medical ambitions and her missionary zeal, they were not pleased with the notion of her piloting aircraft. But while Hanna lost interest in her other career goals, she never gave up on the dream of flying.

Because the Versailles Treaty that ended World War I banned Germany from using powered aircraft, Reitsch had to settle for piloting gliders. As a test pilot for a glider research institute in the 1930s, she made a name for herself by setting altitude and distance records. It was Reitsch who was asked to test a new feature of German aviation—dive brakes. These devices helped to slow down and increase the stability of airplanes during power dives. After Reitsch successfully demonstrated them, they became a standard feature of all military aircraft.

During Germany's military rearming in the 1930s, the intensely patriotic Reitsch was recruited as a test pilot for powered military planes. Her small size (5 feet, 90 pounds) gave her a working advantage in some of the terribly cramped experimental plane cockpits. Although her courage quickly won the respect of her superiors, it nearly got her killed. On one occasion she almost had her head sliced off by a rope while testing ways to restrain aircraft landing on a ship.

On the other hand, the world's first woman test pilot was not about to risk her neck trying to carry out some of her superior's schemes. Preparing for an invasion of Great Britain in 1941, German authorities hatched a plan to tow enormous gliders into the air. Each of these gliders was to carry 200 soldiers. Rockets attached to the wings were supposed to boost these cumbersome transports to their destinations. Reitsch discovered that this jumbo "Gigant," as it was called, was critically underpowered. It handled poorly and often stalled, or dropped in altitude. After barely escaping with her life when she was unable to get one of these contraptions off the ground, she refused to fly any more tests. Her words of warning were ignored until an accident during one training exercise killed 129 glider troops.

While the Me 163B Komet was not exactly reliable either, Reitsch believed the risk of flying it was worth taking. She was one of 42 test pilots selected to fly the new rocket-powered planes being rushed into production. Piloting the Komet was, in her words, "to live a fantasy of Munchhausen." (Baron von Munchhausen was a fictional German character who went through wildly improbable adventures.) She could hardly wait to get into a Komet and feel the roar and the fire and the exhilarating acceleration that could shoot her up to 30,000 feet in just 90 seconds.

Her first mission was to check out the flying abilities of the Komet design in unpowered gliding tests. The first four flights in this program were routine. But on her fifth flight in the Komet, Hanna Reitsch experienced the dark side of test flying. A tow plane pulled her Me 163B down the runway and guided it into the air. After reaching a safe height of about 30 feet, Reitsch pulled the lever to release the takeoff dolly from the underside of the plane.

As the tow plane gained speed, her craft began to shake alarmingly. Reitsch had no idea what was happening until the tow-plane pilot pointed to the bottom of her plane while raising and lowering his own landing gear. He was telling her that the release mechanism had failed, and that she was carrying the heavy dolly along with her. At this point, many pilots might have bailed out; but Reitsch was determined to save the valuable test plane.

Unfortunately, the wind turbulence caused by the undercarriage caused her to lose control as she maneuvered for the landing. At a height of 100 feet, her plane stalled. From there it plummeted and smashed into the earth. Still conscious after the impact, Reitsch was relieved that the plane had not flipped over on its back. Then she noticed the blood gushing from her face and discovered her nose had been sheered off by the impact!

Hanna Reitsch fought off shock long enough to take a pencil and note pad from her pocket and scratch some notes about how the plane had performed before the crash. Her injuries were so massive that she was not expected to live. But after five months in intensive care, she emerged, ready to take to the air again.

## THE THRESHOLD OF SOUND

Through the sacrifices of Reitsch and others, Germany was leading the field in rocket-powered aviation. By July of 1944, Me 163B Komets were streaking into action, flying high above the ceilings of the conventional Allied planes. On July 6, 1944, Rudolf Opitz took off from Peenemünde in a Komet equipped with an extra rocket chamber intended to increase the rocket plane's range. His purpose was merely to test the new equipment, but at about 13,000 feet, the Komet began to surge under the tremendous power of its dual rocket chambers. It climbed more than 1,600 feet in just four seconds, accelerating all the while.

The Komet sped past the maximum speed for which it was designed. Opitz quickly shut off the rocket engine, but it appeared to be too late. The mysterious high-speed forces pushed the nose of his plane toward the ground. Opitz plunged toward the Baltic Sea, his plane spinning out of control. Just before the Komet hit the water, Opitz regained command of the craft and steered it back to his air base.

When he stepped out of the Komet, he saw that his rudder was in tatters, evidence of the invisible force that had held him in its grip. An evaluation of the flight data showed that Opitz had reached a speed of 702 miles per hour before cutting his motor. He had zoomed nearly to the threshold of the speed of sound—far faster than any human had ever traveled before!

The Germans built another rocket plane that might well have tested the sonic wall had it been given a chance. The Bachem BP 20 Natter (the word Natter means "viper") was perhaps the most exotic aircraft design during the war. Not quite 20 feet long, the tiny Natter was a wooden-framed aircraft, designed to be launched from a platform in an almost vertical position. The Natter would be difficult to control and impossible to land. The plan was to have the pilot guide the plane toward the target, fire rocket-powered missiles, and then bail out.

Whether this qualified the Natter as a true airplane is debatable. Nevertheless, wind-tunnel tests with the Natter demonstrated that the craft could travel at 95 percent of the speed of sound without encountering the disastrous effects normally associated with high speed. Had the project been allowed to proceed without interruption, it might well have been a Natter that punched through the sound barrier.

The Natter project, however, was begun too late and doomed to failure. Allied bombs were destroying German factories and airfields involved in the production of the tiny craft. At the beginning of 1945, as Germany's defenses were collapsing on all fronts, panicky government officials rushed the project along. Over the protests of those working on the Natter, a manned test flight was ordered.

Lothar Siebert stepped forward to accept the perilous assignment of piloting that test. On February 28, 1945, he climbed up to the takeoff platform and entered the Natter. Shortly after the rocket engines were ignited, Siebert's Natter blasted off the ground in a sea of black smoke. It climbed rapidly, according to plan, when the canopy suddenly fell off and the Natter flipped onto its back. After climbing a while longer, the plane looped and smashed into the ground, killing Siebert. Eventually several Natters were successfully test-flown, but the project was buried in the chaos that reigned in Germany during the final weeks of the war.

The German achievements in rocket power made it obvious that rocket engines would soon be able to power an airplane at speeds greater than the speed of sound. Rapid improvement in jet engines also gave promise of providing ample power. As far as humans traveling at the speed of sound, there were three key questions. Could this newly developed speed be controlled? If so, who would be the first to conquer the speed of sound? And how many more would die in the attempt?

While the first question was being debated, the front

runners in the race to break the sound barrier were eliminated. Heavy Allied bombing of airfields and factories had hampered and then destroyed Germany's efforts to perfect their rocket planes. Upon surrendering to Allied forces on May 7, 1945, Germany forfeited all its military technological innovations. The Soviet Union, the United States, Great Britain, and others rushed in to obtain German know-how in aviation and to recruit German scientists to head their own projects.

## NARROWING THE COMPETITION

Had the war ended differently, a German pilot would probably have been the first human to pierce the sound barrier. That person could well have been Hanna Reitsch. But she eliminated herself from the competition out of fierce loyalty to her country. American troops occupying Germany at the end of the war offered her a stark choice. She could either take up the United States's offer to join them and choose any test-flight project she wanted, or she could spend her time in prison. Reitsch chose to spend 15 months in prison rather than join the many German aviation and rocket experts who joined foreign research projects. She never worked again as a test pilot and died in 1979 at the age of 67.

The other chief rival that the war eliminated from the speed of sound chase was Japan. With help from their German allies, the Japanese had built rocket planes at the end of World War II. Some of these were kamikaze planes, which were not so much airplanes as piloted bombs. These 20-foot long wooden planes were loaded down with explosives. Carried to the target area by another plane to conserve fuel, three rocket engines launched the kamikaze (Japanese for divine wind) toward the target at about 600 miles per hour.

Since these suicide planes made no attempt to land safely, they cannot really be considered aircraft. The closest Japan came to a true rocket fighter was the Shusui (Sword Wind). Production of this airplane was delayed and nearly stopped when a submarine carrying key German technological information was sunk. Japan carried on using the knowledge that it had. On July 7, 1945, the Japanese were ready to test their rocket fighter. Pilot Toyohiko Inuzuka took off from the Yokosuka airfield and soared into the air at a 45-degree angle.

The Shusui climbed only to 1,300 feet before its rocket engine failed. The rocket plane slowed down rapidly and then stalled. With no power to assist him, Inuzuka sat helplessly as the Shusui dropped straight to the ground and exploded. The war ended before the Japanese could carry out further testing, and the conditions of surrender prevented Japan's participation in high-speed air research.

That narrowed the competitors to three: the Soviet Union, Great Britain, and the United States. No one knew, however, if they were racing for a reasonable goal or whether their pilots were merely rushing headlong into an unbreakable barrier. One thing was certain: the probe into the unknown reaches of speed would continue to be costly. German rocket planes had killed more German pilots during the war than enemy fire. While seeking the secrets of high-speed flight, more test pilots would meet the fate of Inuzuka, Siebert, and Pohl.

# 4

# Great Britain and the Sound Barrier

When the dust had cleared at the end of World War II, Great Britain stood atop the aviation world. Their jets were clearly the fastest operational planes in existence. They had been pushed there by necessity, as their only hope of staving off defeat at the hands of Germany had been the skill and ingenuity of their air force. So, aviation technology had become the country's number one priority. Also, with the United States caught off guard in jet and rocket engine technology and the Soviets lagging in industry, the British had the clearest path to breaking the sound barrier.

British pilots took advantage of these factors to stake their claims as the world's fastest fliers. In light of what we now know about the German rocket planes, the official world records established immediately after the war may seem like a lot of fuss about nothing. But after the secrecy and chaos of the war, it was important to reestablish order and standards to the claims of being the fastest. After all, World War II pilots had frequently made fantastic claims.

For example, there were stories about British pilots diving in Spitfires at speeds far above the recognized world records. There was also a story about Lieutenant Colonel Cass Hough breaking the sound barrier as early as September of 1942. *Newsweek* magazine featured an article about how Hough had challenged the high-speed destructive forces in his P-38 Lightning. Hough climbed to 43,000 feet, pointed the nose down, and opened up his engines to full speed. The plane almost immediately went into the bizarre, uncontrolled spin that other pilots had complained about. According to the account, Hough had hit a top speed of about 780 miles per hour, and had matched this in a similar dive in a P-47 Thunderbolt five months later. If these reports were true, then Cass Hough was the first person to travel at the speed of sound.

Then there was the widely published report of the exploits of Lieutenant Robert Knapp of Norwich, New York, a veteran of more than 80 missions. In October of 1944, Knapp was flying a P-47 Thunderbolt in pursuit of a squadron of German fighters. Knapp went into a power dive, the common method of attack. Starting from a height of about 28,000 feet, he plunged a mile and a half to reach the enemy squadron. But by that time, his controls had locked; and in Knapp's words, the P-47 "started sliding through the air as if on ice." Unable to get the plane to respond to handling, the pilot was ready to bail out. His airspeed indicator, however, showed a speed of about 600 miles per hour, a very dangerous speed for ejecting from a plane.

It was a story familiar to pilots. Knapp kept working the controls, searching for some way to stabilize the plane as the plane kept streaking toward the ground. At about 5,000 feet, the plane finally responded, and Knapp pulled out of the dive.

Knapp's airspeed indicator showed that he had topped out at about 840 miles per hour. If true, that meant that Knapp had not only punched through, but had shattered the sound barrier.

Not suprisingly, the scientific and aviation communities were more skeptical of these reports than were the general media. An article in the October 4, 1944 issue of *Popular Science* magazine stated their "doubt that man has ever closely approached the speed of sound." Experts pointed out that the airspeed indicators in use were not reliable, particularly in high-speed dives. Claims of supersonic flight in diving World War II planes have since been discounted.

Confusion over airplane speeds, especially as they related to the speed of sound, led the British Royal Air Force to perfect the machmeter. This cockpit instrument, named after nineteenth century Austrian physicist Ernst Mach who pioneered a great deal of knowledge about sound waves, was far more accurate. Taking into account that the speed of sound varies with temperature, the machmeter gave the airplane's speed as a percentage of the local speed of sound. In other words, a machmeter reading of Mach .80 indicated that at that altitude and pressure the airplane was traveling at 80 percent of the speed of sound.

With all the stories and rumors floating about, many thought it was time to return to some officially confirmed speeds. Unfortunately, the old restrictions that aviation officials had long relied upon for record attempts were not only restrictive but dangerous. For example, an airplane traveling at 600 miles per hour was courting disaster when flying below the approved height of only 75 meters.

# THE GLOSTER METEORS

Confident that their Gloster Meteor jets were easily faster than any other airplane in production, British pilots set out to claim the speed record shortly after the end of the war. The Meteors used in these speed runs were not regular Meteors but were modified for maximum speed. British squadron leader P. Stanbury set the stage for the British assault with an unofficial clocking of 603 miles per hour on October 19, 1945.

A few weeks later two other British pilots revved up their Meteors to make the speed record the official property of the British Isles. On November 7, a 37-year-old Royal Air Force captain, H. J. "Willie" Wilson, took off into the overcast skies over Herne Bay, near Kent, England. For a while it appeared that poor weather would halt Wilson's attempt. After experiencing difficulty sighting the flares that marked the course, Wilson realized that it would be wise to postpone the run. Gloster Meteors were nothing to fool around with. But at the last minute Wilson changed his mind and decided to run the risk.

Wilson's jet engines proved to be more than up to the task. Staying just within the limits of comfort and control, Wilson held off going at full throttle. His Meteor blazed four runs over the 70-mile course at an average speed of 606 miles per hour.

Eric Greenwood, a 38-year-old civilian pilot for the Gloster Aircraft Company, the builder of the Meteor, went up in the sky right after Wilson's run. Greenwood finished the run with what he thought was a better time than Wilson's mark. Photographic timing, however, which measured speed accurately by recording the plane's progress at precise intervals, demonstrated that he had fallen just short of the record. When notified of the failure, Greenwood's response may have set a world record for grace and sportsmanship. "Really? Good old Willie!" he exclaimed.

Captain E. M. Donaldson continued the British Meteor's postwar dominance the following autumn. Flying over Sussex, England, on September 7, 1946, Donaldson boosted the official record to 616 miles per hour. The British also reported an unofficial test run of 626 miles per hour by yet another Gloster Meteor.

At the same time, British aviation experts were fearful that the Meteor was reaching the limits of safe operation. Although it had proven that it had power to spare, thorough testing indicated that the jet could not withstand the mysterious battering that was to be expected at higher speeds. In order to reach their goal of traveling at the speed of sound, they would have to do more than tinker with the Meteor. They would have to develop something entirely new.

## M52

As early as 1942, British authorities had made a serious run at the sound barrier. With government backing, British engineers set out to build a radically new airplane capable of traveling 1,000 miles per hour. Their latest research indicated that an extremely thin wing could slice through the turbulence at high speed, and reduce many of the most destructive effects of shock waves. The development of improved, high-strength, lightweight metals offered a means of building a strong, razor-edged wing. Accordingly, the British M52 experimental jet, designed and built in secret, was given thin wings to go with a body shaped like a bullet.

Although the basic designs later proved to be sound, the project ran into a nest of problems. Despite painstaking efforts to reinvent an entirely new power system, the initial versions of the M52 could not outrace a conventional, diving Spitfire. Progess was so sluggish and costly that before the end of the war British aviation experts had to conclude that the M52 was not the superspeed plane they had in mind. A Royal Air Force report issued in July of 1944 stated that the goal of supersonic flight was not a realistic goal at this time, and the program was canceled.

The failure of the M52 gave the United States enough time to climb back into the supersonic picture. As American jets and rocket planes finally began to close the gap on the Gloster Meteor in 1946, British hopes for winning the race to the sound barrier were pinned on one man: Sir Geoffrey de Havilland, Sr.

## THE DEMISE OF THE SWALLOW

Geoffrey de Havilland had earned an international repu-tation as a brilliant aircraft designer, a man with ideas and the courage to try them out. Born in 1882, he had shown exceptional engineering creativity at an early age. While attending boarding school, he built his own motorbike, which he used to transport himself home on weekends.

De Havilland earned his living as a bus designer until he became fascinated by the reports from the United States of the Wright brothers' powered flights. The thought of flying, once implanted in de Havilland's mind, virtually crowded out all other interests. He begged his grandfather to lend him enough money so that he could quit his job and begin building his own airplane engine.

Together with his friend, Frank Hearle, de Havilland designed and constructed an airplane out of wire, wood, and linen. The wings were made of fabric stitched together by de Havilland's wife. When the plane was finished in 1909, de Havilland climbed aboard to make his long-awaited dream come true. His moment of triumph lasted only a few seconds, or as long as it took the airplane to lift off the ground, wobble 40 yards, and crash. Undaunted, de Havilland set out to build a better plane with the remainder of the funds from his grandfather.

The incident turned out to be a foreshadowing of his entire career. He would celebrate many triumphant moments, only to encounter failure. From the ruin of one aviation scheme, he would pick up the pieces and start on another. De Havilland finally succeeded in flying at about the time of his first son's birth. (That boy, Geoffrey de Havilland, Jr., would one day find himself tempted by the same lure of the skies that had hooked his father.) But unfortunately, having used up the loan from his grandfather, de Havilland and Hearle had to go back to work.

By the first decade of the 1900s the aviation industry was attracting enough interest so that a clever inventor such as de Havilland who could design and build innovative aircraft was in hot demand. The primary customer for his work was the British government, which was beginning to recognize the military possibilities of the airplane.

Introduced in 1916, the D.H.2 was nearly as primitive a craft as de Havilland's first home-made contraptions. Made of wood, it offered no windshield for the pilot, no parachute, and was not even equipped with brakes. Yet the D.H.2 was a sturdy machine that could fly and maneuver at nearly 100 miles per hour. The D.H.2 was used by the British in World War I in early air combat against Germany. It was quickly replaced by two other de Havilland designs, the D.H.4 and D.H.9, which were the most heavily used Allied planes of the war.

Following the war, Geoffrey de Havilland formed his own aircraft company and made one of the most important contributions to aviation with his production of the two-seat Moth. This design has been likened to the Ford Model T automobile. Both were so inexpensive and simple to operate that they attracted vast numbers of buyers. The Moth was the most successful light airplane in history. It was so well constructed that de Havilland once crashed one on purpose to show that it would not break. Great Britain produced a large number of amateur pilots between the wars, largely because the Moth made flying affordable and undemanding. This fact laid the groundwork for the expanded Royal Air Force that saved Great Britain from disaster in World War II.

The de Havilland company labored feverishly to furnish 23,000 airplanes to the Allied cause in World War II. Their most valuable creation was a fast-flying light bomber. This plane, which became known as the Mosquito, had to be made of wood because of the scarcity of steel in the country. Although bombers are normally built more for carrying capacity than for speed, the Mosquito early in the war could outrun many fighters. It proved especially useful in intercepting German V-1 "buzz bombs." Mosquitos were credited with shooting down 600 of these long-range V-1 missiles in a span of 60 days.

As seems to have been the case with nearly every aviation success, de Havilland's triumphs did not come without steep costs. It had long been a matter of principle to de Havilland that the dangerous first flights in all de Havilland models were to be made by Geoffrey himself. But when age finally took its toll on the master designer, he passed the duty on to his sons. Beginning in 1938, Geoffrey de Havilland, Jr., took over the honors, and it was he who broke in all the de Havilland models manufactured in World

War II. His younger brother John also performed test flights for the family business. In 1943 John de Havilland was test-flying a Mosquito under instructions from his father. The plane collided in midair with another Mosquito, and John joined the long list of test pilots killed in the line of duty.

The elder de Havilland overcame the weight of grief to produce the Vampire, a jet plane that could travel more than 500 miles per hour. After laying the groundwork for the world's first commercial jet liner, he then set his sights on the most tempting prize of all aviation—the speed of sound.

A number of British engineers had concluded that the best way of combating the brutal effects of high-speed turbulence was with swept wings. A swept wing does not stick straight out from the side of the plane as does the conventional wing, but angles back toward the tail. In 1946 de Havilland constructed the D.H. 108, with 40-degree swept wings. Its odd appearance was compounded by the fact that it had no tail, a concession to the theory that some of the high-speed buffeting in a conventional design was caused by the interaction of shock waves between the wings and the tail.

De Havilland had two goals in mind in producing this plane. One was scientific: he wanted to see if proper stability could be achieved with swept wings and the elimi-nation of the tail. His second goal was both personal and patriotic. Great Britain's world-record speed of 616 miles per hour, the badge of British air supremacy, was in danger. Just one week after Captain Donaldson set the mark, a United States Army XP-84 Thunderbolt jet had come within five miles per hour of breaking it. The D.H. 108, dubbed "The Swallow," appeared to offer the best hope of maintaining Great Britain's top ranking in aviation. Perhaps it would also prove to be the design breakthrough that would achieve the dream of traveling at the speed of sound.

Widely considered Great Britain's top test pilot, Geoffrey de Havilland's son was the man who was going to make the run at the world record and probe the forbidden zone at the edge of the speed of sound. During the first trial, in May of 1946, the Swallow performed smoothly. As Geoffrey gradually increased speed, the Swallow handled easily and did everything asked of it. So far, he had prudently held back from approaching the power limits of his jet engine. Once he brought all that power into play, a string of world records should easily be within reach.

On the evening of September 27, 1946, the 37-year-old de Havilland guided his Swallow into the air above the Thames estuary for a practice run. Some say he was flying level, others believe he went into a dive. Either way, he accelerated the plane up to world-record speed to see how it would respond to the mysterious forces.

Some have speculated that Geoffrey de Havilland, Jr., was the first human to cross the sound barrier. While that may be doubtful, he very probably exceeded the official world record of 616 miles per hour. He may even have traveled, for a brief time, faster than any of the German Me 163B Komet pilots. No one knows for certain because no one saw what happened. The last anyone saw of Geoffrey de Havilland, Jr., and the D.H. 108 Swallow they were streaking off into the dusk, "as if a match had been swept across a hot stove lid."

The few pieces of the wreckage that were recovered were the only clues as to what had happened. The evidence showed only that the plane disintegrated, spewing debris far and wide across the countryside. The body was not found for 10 days.

Aviation experts speculated that there was a design problem with the Swallow. The wing tips, it was said, may have been built too close to the plane's center of gravity. This left it vulnerable to the merciless mysterious pounding that all planes experienced as they approached the speed of sound. The best guess was that de Havilland had exceeded Mach .90—90 percent of the speed of sound, and perhaps as high as Mach .94.

No amount of scientific analysis and objective reasoning could ease the psychological impact of the shocking demise of the Swallow. The accident appeared to confirm the worst fears about that unknown phenomena called the sound barrier. It seemed that a pilot might as well try to smash a plane through a concrete wall as try to penetrate this invisible wall in the sky. The de Havilland disaster left vivid evidence of the might of this strange force. Approaching the speed of sound, other planes had been battered, some had been badly damaged, others had spun out of control and crashed. The Swallow, traveling closer yet to the speed of sound, had not merely been twisted. It had not simply crashed. It had been obliterated!

## FLYING STRAW IN A HURRICANE

"Compressibility" was the word the engineers used to describe the frightening barrage of forces that had attacked the Swallow as it approached the speed of sound. Pilots fortunate enough to return from an encounter with compressibility often appeared as though they had entered a world of living nightmares, and their descriptions of what had happened could equal the wildest notions of the best science fiction writers. Perhaps the most colorful was one pilot's statement that trying to fly a plane under the effects of compressibility was like "trying to fly straw in a hurricane."

One look at some of the pilots and their mangled crafts showed that this terrific battering was not merely a product of their imaginations. Many aviators staggered away from their airplanes with swollen ears and eyes, their heads blotched with purple bruises from being slammed around the cockpit. Together with the haunting image of the D.H. 108 being crushed like an eggshell, this conveyed so much emotional drama that it was difficult for a cold, objective analysis of compressibility.

A number of experts had already tried to steer the talk away from an invisible, impenetrable wall in the sky toward a more clinical analysis of the problem. The sound barrier was not a rigid law of nature—the absolute limit of speed beyond which matter could not travel. That kind of thinking had been exploded long before by Carl Gustaf DeLaval, a Swedish inventor with more than 1,000 patents to his credit. Before DeLaval's time, many engineers believed it was impossible to devise a machine that could produce an air current with a velocity greater than the speed of sound. Yet, DeLaval had managed to do so during the latter part of the nineteenth century. He had proved that matter could be made to move faster than the speed of sound.

Since that time, a number of objects had been propelled at speeds greater than sound could travel. Firearms had been developed to discharge bullets at supersonic speeds. Robert Goddard in the mid-1930s had fired a rocket through the air at supersonic speed. German engineers of World War II had refined this science and perfected rockets that could make sound waves look as if they were standing still. The long-range V-2 missiles fired at Great Britain beginning in late 1944 raced toward their targets at 3,500 miles per hour, nearly five times the speed of sound.

Obviously, the sound barrier could not be some sort of invisible force field that automatically destroyed or stopped objects that reached supersonic speed. What, then, were the differences between the missiles that easily pierced the sound barrier and the aircraft that were shaken like rats in a terrier's mouth as they approached the speed of sound? First of all, rockets and bullets were far stronger structures than airplanes. They were dense, solid pieces with no attached appendages. Second, missiles were hurled through the air, pushed forward strictly by their own momentum. Airplanes, by definition, had to be supported by a current of air.

One approach to the problem of compressibility was to make airplanes stronger so that they could withstand the greater stresses that occurred at higher speeds. But structural strength alone would not defeat the sound barrier if something happened at high speeds to disturb the air that supported the airplane's flight.

It was this disturbance of air that lay at the heart of the problem. Air was not something that a plane just cut through smoothly like a hot knife through butter. A moving object disturbed the air that it passed through. At slow speeds, this disturbance was not particularly noticeable. Even at higher speeds, the disturbance appeared to be merely an aftereffect; the moving object left disturbed air in its wake as it passed through. At extremely high velocities, however, the extent of the disturbance was more obvious. So obvious, in fact, that in 1892 Charles Vernon Boys was able to capture it on film.

Boys used high-speed photography to isolate an image of a bullet flying through the air. The photograph clearly showed that the air did not part smoothly as the bullet passed through it. Instead, if formed a series of narrow V-shaped patterns directly in front of the point of the bullet. This was the first evidence that fast-flying objects actually compress the air in front of them as they travel. In basic terms, at extremely high speeds, the air molecules can no longer get out of the way of the object quickly enough. They begin to bunch up. The blunter the point of the object, the greater this compression, which is why missiles are designed with sharp points.

Aviation tests indicated that the air compression at the nose of the airplane caused no insurmountable problem at high speed. After all, missiles and bullets created the same sort of compression without drastic effects. But all kinds of chaos developed around the wings at high speeds. An airplane depended upon the flow of air around the wings to lift and support it. At high speeds, the air was found to bunch up around the wings and formed what were called shock waves. The air that struck these shock waves was not able to slide smoothly around the wing. It could be deflected at any number of angles or could completely change direction. The shock waves broke up the smooth flow of air that was supposed to keep the wings stable, and shot it around every which way.

Physicists' descriptions of the effects of shock waves on the air were as colorful as the stories told by test pilots. One physicist described the situation by saying that it was as though the air was breaking away in chunks, leaving nothing to support the plane. Another said that this disturbance of air left the tail of the plane to "wade through air that looks like Niagara Falls." Still another explained that air traveling at the speed of sound "acts like boiling water."

However it was described, the thing about compressibility was that it made it nearly impossible to fly an airplane. This swirling eddy of air destroyed the lift normally provided by the wings; that was the main reason why high-speed aircraft so frequently started falling like rocks. The tail's rudder and elevator (devices used to change an airplane's direction left and right, up and down, respectively) locked up. The controls froze so that pilots were unable to budge the control stick. Shock waves battered the plane, weakening and sometimes tearing the structure.

Wind-tunnel tests confirmed that the violent effects of shock waves reached their peak when air approached the speed of sound. Wind tunnels would choke up from the turbulence at Mach .96 but would operate again at Mach 1.2. That offered some evidence for the existence of a permanent barrier caused by shock waves that occurred right at the speed of sound. It also held out the hope that once a way was found to cross that barrier, turbulence would no longer be a problem.

On the other hand, aviation experts noted that the air crowding over the curved surfaces of a plane would actually be traveling much faster than the velocity of the plane. Airflow over the wing of a plane flying at 500 miles per hour would reach velocities far greater than 500 miles per hour in relation to the airplane. In other words, some of the high-speed aircraft were already flying in air that was moving at the speed of sound. Perhaps that meant that an aircraft flying at Mach .8 and Mach .9 was experiencing some of the worst effects of shock waves. It was quite possible that improvements in aircraft design were already very close to breaking through the sound barrier.

But no one knew how powerful shock waves could become or whether the air at the speed of sound behaved too erratically to predict. Although stronger materials and construction techniques were being developed, it had not been proven that an airplane could be built strong enough to survive the turbulence.

Even those engineers who believed that the sound barrier would soon be broken tempered their optimism. Some believed that supersonic speeds would be reached, but only when inventors came up with a revolutionary aircraft design. As late as June of 1947 an article in *Popular Science* magazine issued the following warning: "For both humanitarian and scientific reasons, we want the pioneer supersonic pilot to return to earth alive. If he is to do that, there are a lot more answers that must be supplied before take-off."

## UNMANNED EXPERIMENTS

The awesome disintegration of the de Havilland Swallow shook the confidence of test pilots and aeronautical engineers all over the world. All of the effort and expense of building more powerful engines, stronger airplanes, and better controls were a waste of time if the normal laws of physics were suspended at the speed of sound.

The ominous shadow of the Swallow also knocked the wind out of the British high-speed airplane projects. The British decided that the mysterious forces of compressibility were too dangerous. Intimidated by the sound barrier, British researchers decided there was no sense in sacrificing more pilots just to satisfy a scientific curiosity. Instead, they retreated to experiments with unmanned planes operated by remote control.

By the autumn of 1947, British engineers had either finished or were in the process of constructing two dozen specially built remote-control planes. These tiny planes, only 11 feet long with 4-foot wings, were nicknamed "Vickys." They were designed to reach a top speed of 900 miles per hour in level flight, well beyond the speed of sound. In October, one of these experimental craft was carried to a height of 36,400 feet by a de Havilland Mosquito and cut loose.

The Vicky dove sharply to pick up speed. When the controllers tried to pull it out of the dive, the Vicky did not respond. Spewing thick black smoke, the little plane flew unsteadily into cloud cover at 10,000 feet and was never seen again. As with the Swallow, there was speculation that the Vicky had passed through the speed of sound, but there was no confirmation of it.

Great Britain's cautious, unmanned approach to the sound barrier progressed too slowly to have any impact on high-speed aviation. By the time of the first Vicky flight, the British had given up the lead in the race to crack the sound barrier.

The Wright brothers' pioneering flight of 1903 inspired aviation enthusiasts and scientists to test the barriers to speed in flight.

The planes of the early twentieth century were delicate and often odd-looking contraptions. Louis Blériot's craft broke records for speed at the 1909 air show in Reims, France.

American scientist Robert Goddard advanced rocket technology almost single-handedly.
Goddard launched the world's first liquid-propellant rocket in 1926.

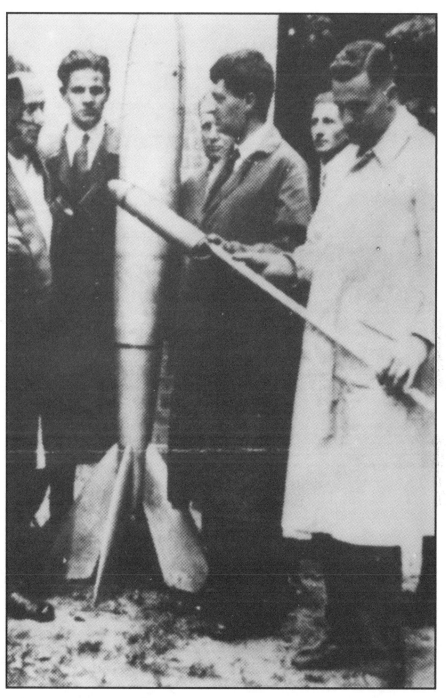

Wernher von Braun, holding rocket, was one of the German scientists who worked to equip fighter planes with liquid fuel rockets. The goal—greater and greater speed!

The German Messerschmitt Komet flown by Rudolf Opitz. The Komet was a volatile rocket-plane, loaded with explosive fuel and equipped with skids for landing.

The Natter hardly looked like an airplane with its stubby wings and long, blunt nose. In fact, it was designed to be launched in a vertical position, like a rocket. Despite its ungainly appearance, the Natter was tested for traveling at 95 percent of the speed of sound.

Hanna Reitsch was a test pilot for Nazi Germany's Komet program. Here, she accepts honors from Adolf Hitler and German air minister Hermann Göring.

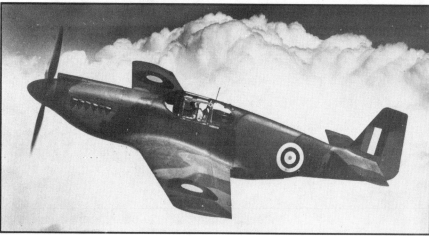

(OPPOSITE PAGE) The German Focke-Wulf 190, top, the American Mustang, center, and the British Supermarine Spitfire, below, were among the fastest planes of the 1940s.

Geoffrey de Havilland, Sr. was one of Britain's foremost airplane designers. His designs included the Moth (shown in the background of this portrait), the Mosquito, and the Swallow.

*(Opposite Page)* The Swallow. Geoffrey de Havilland, Jr., perished while pushing this plane towards a world speed record.

*(Top)* The bullet-shaped X-1 was Bell Aircraft's hope for shattering the sound barrier.

*(Left)* Test pilot Chuck Yeager, helmet grasped under one arm, holds on to the cockpit of the X-1.

A B-29 bomber releases the tiny X-1 for a test run. "Just a matter of flying the airplane" was Chuck Yeager's laconic reply after having broken the sound barrier.

# 5
## *The New Challenger*

$G$reat Britain's disappointing supersonic efforts left the door open for the United States and the Soviet Union. While secret projects were being run in the Soviet Union, most attention was focused on the Americans as they prepared for an all-out assault on the sound barrier.

The United States had arrived late on the scene in rocket and jet research. The first major government sponsored effort came in September of 1942, several years after German jets and rocket planes had been successfully tested. At that time, John Northrop, president of Northrop Aircraft Incorporated, laid out a radical plan before the United States Army Air Force. His idea, which he had been privately exploring since the 1920s, was to build a rocket-propelled fighter plane with virtually no body. He proposed having the pilot lie on his stomach so that the center of the plane did not need to be much thicker than the wings.

This "flying wing," Northrop reasoned, offered a number

of advantages. It should be better able to cut through the turbulent air at high speeds and minimize the stress on the aircraft body caused by sudden high-speed turns. A flying wing would also provide a very small target for enemy gunners. In addition, a pilot in a prone position should be able to withstand greater forces of acceleration than a sitting one. This was not a particularly comfortable position for flying, but the situation was eased somewhat by a head support for the pilot.

The Air Force approved Northrop's plan for the XP-79, a plane with a 36-foot wingspan. American rocket technology was still so primitive that the Air Force did not care to have the entire project depend on rocket power. The United States had not advanced very far in jet research either. Hedging their bets, the Air Force commissioned two versions of the XP-79—one powered by a rocket and one powered by a jet.

Northrop's proposal was far ahead of existing American technology. There were numerous delays as engineers struggled to find ways of meeting the requirements of this new plane. Most of the problems were with the rocket motors, although there were also difficulties in finding a workable wheel base for takeoff. It was not until October of 1943 that a pilot first took off in a smaller, engineless version of the anticipated XP-79. At this point, as the prototype of the XP-79 was given the new designation of MX-324, the history of the flying wing becomes confusing.

One early test flight of the MX-324 nearly ended in disaster. While banking steeply in the engineless craft, the pilot accidently released the cockpit escape hatch. The craft turned upside down, leaving him hanging in his harness beneath the plane. After a great struggle, the pilot managed to pull himself onto the center section, slide off one wing, and parachute to safety.

A rocket motor was installed in the MX-324 in late spring of 1944. On the morning of July 5, Northrop test pilot Harry Crosby crawled into the flying wing on his stomach and positioned his head into the padded chin rest. The craft was towed to an altitude of 8,000 feet and then set loose. Crosby fired the engines, and riding a tail of smoke and fire, accelerated to 270 miles per hour before his fuel ran out.

Although considered a brilliant concept and design, Northrop's XP-79 paid the price for the United States' tardy entry into rocket science. The rocket engines that were supposed to power the craft failed miserably. Even though the flying wing flew well in several tests, it showed no promise of reaching the 500 mile-per-hour speeds that were expected of it, that were being easily achieved by German rocket aircraft. Within a few weeks of Harry Crosby's first successful test flight, the rocket-powered XP-79 project was abandoned.

That left only the jet-powered version to save the day for the flying wing. By the time the XP-79B version of the high-speed fighter was ready for testing, World War II was over. Although the immediate need for the plane was past, Harry Crosby was called upon to test the plane on September 12, 1945. Taking off from Muroc Flight Test Base in California, Crosby flew the craft for 14 minutes without incident.

But while performing a slow roll at 7,000 feet, the XP-79B spun out of control. At about 2,000 feet, Crosby bailed out; however, he was apparently struck by his own whirling craft and knocked out before he could open his parachute.

Another pilot had been killed in the quest for speed. The

accident, caused by a malfunctioning control, helped bring Northrop's exotic experiment to an abrupt end. The United States was to remain without a successful jet or rocket-powered aircraft for use during World War II.

## JET OR ROCKET?

During the grimmest days of World War II, mounting evidence of the gap between the Germans and the United States in aviation technology prompted concern among the United States' National Advisory Committee for Aeronautics (the NACA, which later became NASA, the National Aeronautics and Space Administration). After discussing the situation with British experts in 1943, NACA called a conference to address problems that American manufacturers were experiencing in improving high-speed aircraft design. It was pointed out that data being gleaned from wind-tunnel experiments was not enough; high-speed test flights were also needed. From that conference came the idea of following the British plan to produce an experimental airplane that could fly at or above the speed of sound.

That was more or less what Ezra Kotcher, an engineer working at Wright Field in Dayton, Ohio, had proposed back in 1939. Now that the government was finally interested, Kotcher renewed his work on high-speed flight. According to his research, the goal of supersonic flight could best be achieved with rocket power.

Other engineers argued, however, that jet power was the way to go. With the backing of the NACA, the Navy eventually chose to undertake a high-speed flight program using the jet engine. The Air Force, a branch of the Army, moved ahead with Kotcher's proposal.

Regardless of which approach the United States took, it

had the advantage of owning a piece of land that one veteran test pilot called "God's gift to the Air Force." The Muroc Army Air Base was located next to Rogers Dry Lake, 65 miles north of Los Angeles in the Mojave Desert. Rogers Dry Lake was roughly seven miles long by three miles wide. The clay ground was smooth, as level as a pool table, and except for brief periods when rain turned it into a giant ankle-deep puddle, hard as a highway.

No precision was required to land on Rogers Dry Lake. There was no danger of overshooting the landing area even at the high touchdown speeds required for these experimental models. During the first five years after World War II more than 300 emergency landings were made on the lake. The United States military was able to perform a great many tests at Muroc that they could not have tried at a normal airfield, knowing that the lake provided an extra margin of safety.

Jet power brought the United States its first high-speed triumph of the postwar period. On June 19, 1947, about nine months after Great Britain's efforts were virtually frozen by the de Havilland tragedy, a United States pilot claimed the official speed record for the first time in 24 years. Forty-year-old Colonel Albert Boyd, a veteran pilot who had survived two crash landings in his career, roared over Muroc in a modified Lockheed P-80R Shooting Star. This specially designed, thin-winged jet averaged 623.8 miles per hour over a three-kilometer course.

Boyd's achievement was followed by a flurry of new records produced by the Navy's experimental high-speed jets, known as the Douglas D-558 Skystreak series. On August 20, Colonel Turner Caldwell, Jr., of Arlington, Virginia, took off over Muroc and erased Boyd's mark with an average of 640.7 miles per hour, including a best run of

653.4 with the wind behind him. Five days later, Major Marion Carl of the U.S. Marines (a branch of the Navy) erased the old mark with an average speed of 650.6 in his Skystreak.

Yet as rapidly as the United States was setting records, it was not fast enough for United States military authorities. Although the Nazi military machine had been destroyed, many were leery of a new potentially hostile threat—the Soviet Union. The Soviets kept their aviation tests highly secret, but rumors leaked out from reliable sources that the Soviets possessed a jet capable of outrunning any of the American models. *Aviation* magazine reported in May of 1947 that the Soviets had used confiscated German technology to build a plane that had already topped 660 miles per hour.

Already smarting from withering congressional attacks on their tardiness in moving into jets and rockets, United States military officials were determined to beat the Soviets, as well as everyone else, to the sound barrier. They placed most of their hopes on the Air Force's rocket-powered program and an orange, needle-nosed craft designated the XS-1.

# X-1

On March 16, 1945, the United States military awarded the contract for their XS-1 to the Bell Aircraft Corporation of Buffalo, New York. XS-1 (standing for "Experimental Supersonic Number 1") eventually was shortened to X-1.

Writing many years after supersonic speed became commonplace, one aviation historian stated that once the causes and effects of shock waves were understood, "It was relatively simple to design a proper plane with virtually no effects." Not enjoying the benefit of hindsight, the engineers working on the X-1 hardly considered it an easy task. The mysterious, deadly barrier in the sky cast a grim shadow over every task they undertook.

The "relatively simple" matter of designing a proper plane involved the combined efforts of great engineers, including Kotcher, Lawrence Bell, Robert Woods, Paul Emmons, and others. First of all, there was the matter of strength. The basic shape of the X-1 body was patterned after a .50 caliber bullet, an object that was known to have reached supersonic speed. The fuselage was constructed of high-strength aluminum built to withstand an enormous pounding of up to 18 times the force of gravity. The sonic data on which the design of the X-1 was based was obtained by mounting a small half body over the wing of a P-51 and then diving the P-51.

The Bell Aircraft Corporation shied away from the swept-wing concept that de Havilland had tried in the Swallow and instead used conventional, straight-out wings. Wind-tunnel tests had repeatedly confirmed that thin wings could delay and even reduce the effects of shock-wave turbulence. The X-1 was equipped with the thinnest wings possible, at considerable risk to the pilot. A person could not parachute out the side of the plane for fear of being sliced in half by the sharp edges. The X-1's tail was also raised to keep it out of the way of the turbulence swirling back from the wings. The X-1 had an all-moving tail, and elevators and other control devices were improved to ease the problems encountered by other pilots in high-speed flight.

The United States was still feeling its way around as far as rocket engines were concerned, and there was some problem finding a workable one for the X-1. After some false starts, Bell settled on a four-chamber motor produced by Reaction Motors, Inc. This engine went back to the concept of one of the earlier German models, using a combination of liquid oxygen (LOX) and water-alcohol as the energy source. Although the final X-1 design could carry only half the fuel as originally planned, project engineers decided it would have to be enough.

Building a supersonic aircraft presented a multitude of problems that had nothing to do with power, structure strength, or stability. The X-1 would be flying in extremely thin air, and so the pilot needed a supply line of oxygen. Since pure oxygen is highly flammable and a jet engine produces a great deal of flame, this system would have to be carefully designed to insure the pilot's safety. Also, scientists were beginning to understand that prolonged periods of vibration and noise could wear down a pilot's nerves and make him unable to think quickly; so those two elements needed to be reduced as much as possible.

The finished X-1 product was a bright orange and white, bullet-shaped, needle-nosed aircraft, not quite 11 feet high, nearly 31 feet long with a 28-foot wingspan. Whoever piloted the craft would be squeezed into a tiny cockpit, surrounded by recording instruments. He would be sitting atop a powder keg of 465 gallons of liquid oxygen and 498 gallons of alcohol that would be used so quickly by the engine that it would be totally consumed in two and a half minutes of full power.

## JACK WOOLAMS: FIRST X-1 PILOT

A poster displayed in the pilots' preparation room at Muroc Army Air Field (later renamed Edwards Air Force Base) in the mid-1940s heightened the test-pilots' image as steel-nerved, action-loving spirits who laughed in the face of death. The last thing many of the Muroc pilots saw before stepping out to perform a dangerous mission were the words on the poster: "Don't take life too seriously, you'll never get out of it alive anyhow!"

It was an image that Jack Woolams, chief test pilot for Bell Aircraft, fought hard to dispell. Not that Woolams couldn't tell some true-life piloting stories that would make the listener's hair stand on end. In January of 1945, Woolams was asked to dive straight down toward the ground in the United States' first jet-propelled fighter plane. By this time there was not a pilot around who didn't know that the demons of compressibility were waiting for anyone who tried a stunt like that. Predictably, Woolams's controls locked up. At about 600 miles per hour the tail of his plane folded up like tinfoil in a vise. Woolams tried to pull out and the jet bottomed out and jumped into the air, pitching and sliding out of control.

Woolams attempted to bail out, but the canopy over his cockpit was jammed. With just seconds left before he hit the ground, the 6-foot, 170-pound Woolams stood up in the cramped cockpit and strained at the hatch with every ounce of strength left in him. Finally, he cracked the hatch open just in time to abandon the dying plane. The jet was falling so fast that his boots were blown off by the force of the wind. Woolams landed in his stocking feet in six feet of snow and freezing temperatures near Niagara Falls. Only a quick rescue by helicopter saved his life. Unfazed by the experience, Woolams was able to describe for the engineers exactly what had gone wrong in his flight. Two weeks later, he was back in the Bell jet fighters, taking one to the astounding height of over 47,000 feet.

Although Woolams could match any pilot in courage and

skill, he avoided the expected bravado in talking about the X-1. As a married, 29-year-old father of three, he was not interested in taking foolish chances just to feed his ego or get some thrills. In an article he wrote for *Colliers* magazine, Woolams tried to downplay some of the hoopla surrounding the assault on the sound barrier. "Breaking the sound barrier will not be a one-man, devil-may-care side show," he said. Instead, he pointed out that the X-1 involved step-by-step programming—each step carefully planned and practiced, every detail worked out by trained professionals. The approach described by Woolams was logical and scientific, not bold and spectacular. The project would progress as slowly as necessary in order to make sure it was done safely. The X-1 team was going to find out all they could about shock waves before going high in the sky to challenge them.

On January 25, 1946, Woolams took the first small, careful step in bringing the X-1 up to speed. He took an engineless version of the X-1 into the air over Pinecastle Field near Orlando, Florida. After being towed to 25,000 feet, Woolams was set free. He glided slowly downward, familiarizing himself with the cockpit and getting a feel for handling the plane. After satisfying himself that the X-1 was airworthy, he came in for an easy 125 mile-per-hour landing. Woolams made a total of 10 glides in the X-1 before the project was allowed to proceed to its next stage.

While the X-1's engine was being installed that summer, Woolams studied all known aspects of high-speed flight. A plan was developed that called for Woolams to fly at around 530 miles per hour in initial tests and gradually increase speed each flight until he reached 1,000 miles per hour. The pilot voiced confidence in his engineers who assured him that the plane was fast enough and strong enough to break through the sound barrier. Woolams assured the public that the X-1 was actually a very simple plane. In his report after the first glide, Woolams wrote, "Of all the airplanes the writer has flown . . . it is the most delightful one to fly of them all." The only concession he made to the risk involved was a sort of offhand admission that "there will, of course, be some danger. . . . But we are well prepared."

During the month of August, while waiting for the rocket engine to be installed in the X-1, Woolams and two other Bell test pilots, Alvin "Tex" Johnston and Chalmers "Slick" Goodlin, traveled to Cleveland, Ohio. The Bell Aircraft Corporation was entering two of their new supercharged P-39 Airacobras in the Thompson Trophy air race. Woolams was not one to pull rank on his associates. The three pilots flipped coins to see who would pilot the two planes. Goodlin lost, and Woolams and Johnston took to the air. On August 29, 1946, Woolams placed second in qualifying heats and returned to Niagara Falls to have a new motor installed in his plane.

Competing in the air race may have been considered relatively tame compared with Woolams's work in attacking the sound barrier. But there are no certainties for those who whip around the skies at high speed. On August 30, Woolams crashed into Lake Ontario while testing the engine. The man who had been so thoroughly prepared to break the sound barrier died instantly.

## SLICK GOODLIN

The loss of Jack Woolams dealt a severe blow to the X-1 program. Bell had been counting so heavily on their chief pilot that they even custom-designed the cockpit to fit Woolams's dimensions. But the quest for speed seldom stopped long to mourn the passing of those lost along the way. Bell had to decide which of their second-line pilots was to take up the mantle of the supersonic program. Tex Johnston, who had won the air race in Cleveland, was promoted to fill Woolams's position as Bell's chief test pilot. But the honor of taking the X-1 into supersonic flight was given to Slick Goodlin, a twenty-three-year-old pilot with seven years of flying experience.

As his nickname suggests, Slick Goodlin was in many ways the direct opposite of Jack Woolams. While Woolams tried to downplay the hazards of the X-1 and portrayed himself as just one of many professional technicians doing his job, Goodlin possessed a flair for the dramatic. It did not bother him one bit to be cast as America's handsome knight in shining armor, riding off to joust with the deadly dragons of the sound barrier. In fact, he was as much tempted by the lure of Hollywood as he was by the challenges of flying.

Chalmers Goodlin first encountered airplanes at the age of 16 while working on the family farm near Greensburg, Pennsylvania. Pilots taking off from a nearby airport occasionally entertained themselves by swooping down on unsuspecting victims and "buzzing" them. A farm boy milking cows was an inviting target for these antics. Goodlin became so intrigued with the idea of flying that he got a job washing airplanes at that airport. Slick learned to fly and then joined the Royal Canadian Air Force in World War II, prior to the entry of the United States. After spending two years flying British Spitfires against the Germans, he transferred to the U.S. Navy. Following the war, Goodlin joined Bell Aircraft as a test pilot. In those days, most aircraft companies employed their own civilian pilots even on contracts for the military, and these civilians were paid generously for their dangerous work.

When given the job as the X-1 pilot, Slick Goodlin made the most of his celebrity status. His pictures that appeared in the press could easily have been mistaken for movie-star promotions. The public image of Slick Goodlin was a man with his hair stylishly slicked back, dressed in the latest fashion, clenching an expensive pipe between his straight white teeth. He admitted to neither fear nor even nervousness about his serious mission.

Goodlin was a bachelor who took pride in an elegant lifestyle. He drove flashy cars and kept himself in trim condition by swimming every day. Lest anyone suspect Goodlin of being a shallow playboy, he was careful to inform the media that he liked to relax by listening to classical music and reading novels.

Sometimes it seemed as if Slick Goodlin's purpose in life was to live out everyone's childhood dreams. But being young, handsome, and at the throttle of the world's fastest airplane apparently was not enough of a thrill for Goodlin. He once stated that his chief ambition in life was to explore the Amazon jungle in a helicopter.

Even the life of a X-1 pilot, as Woolams certainly would have pointed out, had its dull moments. Rather than let the drama of the X-1 fade, Goodlin used his storytelling skills to keep the public paying attention. Despite the fact that he was performing primarily routine tests in the initial stages of the project, Goodlin usually came back with a good story. He wasn't above embellishing the story and polishing his own image. Once he told newspaper reporters that "the plane was so sensitive that I had to handle the controls like a surgeon."

Goodlin's vivid accounts made even nonfliers wish that they could trade places with him even for a day. "I knew I was moving when I saw the B-29 back up on me," he once told a group of reporters. "But it was so quiet, I could hear the clock tick on my instrument panel."

Yet, Goodlin was far more than just a carefree stage show. He was an excellent pilot and he worked hard on the X-1 project. His daily routine included rigorous workouts in a vibrating, wooden mock-up of the X-1, so he could get accustomed to the tremendous buffeting that he was expected to experience.

And of course, there were real emergencies even in the most carefully planned program. Goodlin's most harrowing moment was when something went wrong with the X-1's cabin pressure, and he was squeezed by nearly bone-crushing forces.

But underneath external appearances, Goodlin was the same mixture of confidence and caution as his predecessor. He was in awe of the incredible power he felt bursting in the engines behind him. And like Woolams he expressed faith in the plane and the project. ("I think it will fly 1,000 miles per hour and I think I'll live through it.") At the same time, he was in no hurry to meet up with the sound barrier. Goodlin's original contract spelled out that he was under no obligation to go any faster than Mach .82 in the X-1, unless he decided it was safe to do so.

After reaching that goal in early 1947, he paused to consider just what was being asked of him. At that point Goodlin decided that if he was going to take the X-1 all the way to the sound barrier, he ought to be well-paid for it. Despite what Woolams had said, this was one of the biggest gambles in aviation history. If the sound barrier were nothing more than a mirage, as some dared to suggest, then why did Bell Aircraft guarantee the structure of the plane only to Mach .82? Why did the *Toronto Star* report, "There is at least an even chance that the plane will break up"? In addition to being asked to fly into unknown territory, Goodlin would be traveling so fast that there would be no hope of bailing out should any problems develop.

Slick Goodlin, who had gained some negotiating experience bargaining with Hollywood producers, weighed all the factors and set his asking price at $150,000. Furthermore, he wanted some of the money deferred in order to shield it from taxes.

It was an unheard of sum for a test pilot. The Air Force, which was paying for the X-1 program, balked at spending that kind of money. After a few unsuccessful attempts at negotiating with Goodlin, the Air Force commanders reached a decision: Why should they negotiate with an overpriced, headline-hogging civilian pilot when they had their own test pilots who would take orders, keep quiet about the project, and fly for a tiny fraction of that pay?

By cutting Goodlin out of the X-1 program, the United States Air Force made one of the most effective budget-cutting moves of all time. The man who took his place at the controls of the world's fastest plane accepted the job in exchange for his regular pay as a captain in the Army Air Force—$283 a month.

Slick Goodlin's salary demands cost him the chance of a lifetime. Another top-flight pilot had been poised on the edge of the supersonic frontier only to have it all slip away. Goodlin disappeared from center stage and went on to work as a Hollywood scriptwriter. But he had lost forever the chance to go down in history as the person who broke the sound barrier, thereby ushering in the space age.

# 6
# *Chuck Yeager*

Colonel Albert Boyd, the man in charge of pushing the X-1 program, kept his doubts to himself. But his actions gave a clue as to what he thought of the risks involved in flying the X-1. In selecting the new pilot for the program, Boyd was looking for another bachelor. Far better to have a lone, unattached pilot smash himself on the sound barrier than a person with a family to support. Boyd was not alone in second-guessing whether the X-1 could break through. The severe buffeting that had rocked Goodlin at speeds well below the sound barrier had dampened others' optimism in the project. Wind-tunnel test data was not encouraging either. One series of results even appeared to indicate that the X-1 would be uncontrollable at the speed of sound.

In May of 1947 Boyd called a meeting of Air Force test-flight pilots and asked for volunteers to take Goodlin's spot at the throttle of the X-1. Some of the pilots had been warned away from the project by their friends in flight engineering. Only eight or so raised their hands. When Boyd analyzed the skills of the volunteers, as well as the records of all 125 pilots in the flight-test section, he saw that he was not going to get his wish. He had a responsibility to the Air Force to get the best man for the job—and that man was a 24-year-old, married man with two children—Charles "Chuck" Yeager.

Yeager had little in common with either of the first two X-1 pilots. He showed neither the detached, reserved professionalism of Woolams nor the suave glitter of Goodlin. Yeager was a tough, fun-loving ex-maintenance man, so unpolished that his superiors considered providing him with English language lessons.

Charles Yeager was born on February 13, 1923, in Myra, West Virginia. The second of five children born to Albert and Susie Mae Yeager, Chuck moved with his family when he was three to the town of Hamlin, located so deep in the backwoods of West Virginia that Yeager liked to claim that "they had to pump daylight in."

It was not a prosperous section of the country, and those people fortunate enough to hold jobs earned their money with their hands. Albert Yeager worked for the railroad and as a gas driller in the coalfields. Exceptionally clever with machinery he could fix just about any piece of equipment ever invented. Albert's mechanical aptitude was passed on to his son. As a young boy, Chuck could take apart and reassemble motors as easily as if they were building blocks.

Upon graduating from Hamlin High School in 1941, Chuck had no real ambitions other than to have a good time with his buddies and hunt in the West Virginia hollows. But with the world torn apart by war, Yeager decided he should enlist in the armed forces. His mind had always been intrigued by the workings of the airplane, so he signed up for a two-year hitch in the Army Air Corps as an airplane mechanic.

As the United States was drawn into World War II, there was an urgent demand for more pilots. Yeager seemed an unlikely candidate to fill the need. Once he had ridden with an officer who was test-flying a plane that Yeager had serviced. They were barely off the ground when Yeager became sick all over the backseat. Yet, Yeager saw the flight program as a way to escape the mundane duties of a mechanic, as well as a quicker way to advance in rank. The benefits seemed worth the discomfort they might cost, so he volunteered for training. Promptly he got sick on his first flights. His first solo flight was also shaky and he landed roughly. But after a while the queasiness stopped and he eventually advanced to the head of his class.

Nevertheless, Yeager's reckless confidence nearly disqualified him from advanced training as a fighter pilot. One night while on guard duty out in the Arizona desert, he decided to relieve the tedium by showing another soldier how to shoot a .30-caliber machine gun. Firing toward some horses that he thought were well out of range, he shot one. In the uproar that followed, Yeager was court-martialed. In the confusion of the early days of war, however, Yeager's records got left behind and the incident was forgotten, until he was already on his way to combat.

As serious as the incident in Arizona had been, it did not cure Yeager's thirst for adventure and mischief. While stationed in Ohio, the young pilot decided to "buzz" his hometown of Hamlin. At seven in the morning, he roared out of the sky and flew down Main Street with the plane's throttle wide open. The local residents, Yeager's parents among them, were furious. But Chuck kept buzzing Hamlin whenever he got the chance.

On another occasion, a friend mentioned that he wanted to cut down one of the trees on his property. Yeager promptly dove his plane at the tree and sheered off the top with his wing tip. When maintenance officers discovered the dented wing full of tree bark, Yeager got another tongue-lashing.

More trouble followed when Yeager could not resist dropping in on a training session at a rival base. After diving through the formation and scattering the planes, he returned to his home base, followed closely by an irate colonel. The colonel screamed at Yeager and ripped into every officer on the base for allowing an irresponsible clown like Yeager to fly.

It was not all fun and games in fighter school, though. As a young pilot, Yeager quickly became acquainted with the unforgiving nature of flying. During six months of fighter training in Nevada, thirteen of his classmates were killed in flying accidents. Yeager had his own close brush with death late in the training program. During a simulated attack, Yeager heard an explosion in the back of the plane. Amid the swirl of smoke and flames, he could see pieces of his aircraft flying in all directions. Traveling at nearly 400 miles per hour, he jumped out of the plane and was knocked unconscious when his chute snapped open. Fortunately, he survived the incident with a fractured back.

## WORLD WAR II ACE

Before being shipped over to England to fight in 1944, Yeager began courting eighteen-year-old Glennis Dick-house, from Oroville, California, where Yeager was based for a time. When he landed in England, Yeager left no doubt as to how he felt about her. He named his P-51 Mustang combat plane *Glamorous Glennis.*

On his seventh mission, over the skies of England Yeager shot down his first enemy aircraft. The very next day he flew with a bomber escort group cruising over northern France. Flying at the tail end of the formation, he was first in line when a squadron of German fighters dove at them from the sky above. Just as Yeager turned to meet the attack, .20-millimeter cannon fire tore into his P-51 Mustang. The engine burst into flames and the dying Mustang spun out of control. Yeager crawled out just in time, and parachuted to Earth, his hands and feet ripped by shrapnel.

He was found by French resistance fighters who hid him in a barn. The Germans came looking for him and even plunged their bayonets into the haystack in which he was hiding. But he escaped and eventually made his way across France, eluding German patrols. After crossing the freezing, snow-covered Pyrenees Mountains, he arrived safely in Spain.

Allied pilots who were shot down over enemy territory and helped back to freedom were not allowed to return to combat flight. They knew too much about the underground resistance movements and might give those secrets away if they were shot down again and captured. But Yeager was not about to go home, and he argued his case all the way up to the commanding officer of the United States, General Dwight Eisenhower. Eisenhower was won over by the young man's fighting spirit and bent the rules to let him stay.

Defying superstition, Yeager gave his next plane the same *Glamorous Glennis* label that he had given to the one that had been shot down. In the final months of the war, Yeager was a terror in the skies. Having Yeager in the flight pattern was extra insurance for pilots. He was blessed with such extraordinary eyesight that he could spot enemy aircraft when those around him could see only empty skies. Yeager also had quick reflexes, and instinctive ability, and he knew what to do in combat. On October 12, 1944, he challenged and knocked out five German fighters in succession. The next month, he became one of the few American airmen to down an Me-262 jet. Altogether, Yeager destroyed 13 enemy aircraft.

## AIR FORCE TEST PILOT

Yeager decided to stay in the Army Air Force after the war in Europe was over. He married Glennis and reported to Wright Field in Dayton, Ohio. All of the Air Force test pilots were college graduates, and most of them had some background in engineering. Despite his impressive war record, the best assignment the high-school educated Yeager could draw was flying repaired aircraft to see if they had been made airworthy. For a person who loved to fly as much as Yeager, it turned out to be a wonderful job. He was in the air six to eight hours every day and flew everything in the Air Force inventory, including captured German and Japanese planes. He even got a chance to take up the United States's first jet fighter.

While he loved the work, it was too much for a man of Yeager's daring and competitive spirit to sit back and watch the hotshot test pilots carve their arcs through the sky. Yeager often flew up to 15,000 feet and waited for them to take their planes up. Then he would dive down at them and "wax their fannies" by flying close in on their tails as if he were going in for a kill. None of the pilots could shake him. But these displays of acrobatic dogfighting did little for his career, only grating on the ample egos of America's best test pilots.

Yeager's lucky break came with the arrival of the Lockheed P-80 Shooting Star. This jet, which was rapidly proving itself the fastest flying machine in the world, also happened to be extremely temperamental. The engines burned out so often that Shooting Stars were forever being dragged into the maintenance hangar. When the repairs were finished, it was Yeager's job to check them out. With the rate at which P-80s were breaking down, Yeager quickly logged more flying time on the jet than anyone else in the Air Force.

The P-80 was tricky to handle. Pilots said that it was like learning to ride a horse after a lifetime of riding elephants. Yeager's skill at handling the P-80 caught the notice of Colonel Boyd. Boyd recognized a gifted flyer when he saw one; furthermore, he was impressed by Yeager's mechanical ability. It was a rare pilot who actually understood every bolt of every engine in every plane he flew. Boyd also thought it was significant that when Yeager piloted the Shooting Star in air shows around the country, he flew so skillfully that he did not blow the engine and leave it stranded 1,000 miles from home, as many other test pilots did. Although it was not a part of any official record, Boyd was also aware that this maintenance pilot was flying circles around his best test pilots in those unscheduled dogfights. So in January of 1946, the colonel invited Yeager to join the ranks of the elite Army Air Force test pilots.

Yeager always seemed to thrive on the very lip of danger and on the ragged edge of the rules. As in his earlier flying days, his chirpy confidence nearly cost him his job. While flying with his instructor over rural Ohio, Yeager's engine blew apart. The pilot had the choice of bailing out or trying an emergency landing. He opted for landing in one of two farm fields. But the plane was falling too fast for Yeager to make it to his chosen field. He smashed through a chicken house, clipped a smokehouse, and damaged the porch of a farmhouse. In the investigation that followed, Yeager's reputation for hotdogging nearly did him in. A witness claimed that Yeager had been showboating down Main Street of a nearby town just before the accident. Fortunately, he had flight instruments on board that showed what he had been doing, and Yeager was off the hook.

## THE LATEST SACRIFICE?

When the Air Force announced it was replacing Goodlin in the X-1, nearly everyone expected the assignment to go to one of the senior test pilots, most likely Major Ken Chilstrom, head of the fighter test section. The choice of Yeager caught them all by surprise and fanned the flames of jealousy that Yeager had earlier kindled among other pilots. But Boyd was not looking at résumés. From personal observation, he knew that no one could match Yeager when it came to flying ability and staying calm in an emergency.

Many of the Air Force engineers thought Yeager was being served up as the latest sacrifice to the obsession with the sound barrier. During the haggling over Slick Goodlin's contract, Bell Aircraft's Tex Johnston had taken the X-1 for a ride to near Mach .80 and emerged with a sober assessment: any man who would risk his life taking the X-1 up to the speed of sound deserved $150,000.

Yeager did not know enough about physics to know if there was such a thing as a sound barrier or not. But he did trust the judgment of his friend Captain Jack Ridley. A small, wiry former wrestler from Oklahoma, Ridley was a brilliant student of the science of flight. In many an engineering class, Yeager had been totally baffled by a concept, only to have Ridley explain the concept in clear, simple terms. Yeager freely admitted that Ridley's explanations were what got him through the classroom portion of flight school. Ridley shrugged off the compliment, noting that Yeager's grasp of the material was uncanny for someone without a college education. "He blots up the stuff as fast as it's poured."

When Colonel Boyd asked who Yeager wanted for flight engineer on the X-1 project, Yeager immediately nominated Jack Ridley. Now he was counting on his Oklahoma friend to get him through the most dangerous assignment of his life. Ridley threw himself into an analysis of all the factors involved. When Bell officials briefed Yeager at their Niagara Falls plant on the X-1 project, Ridley scribbled notes furiously. After sifting through all the information, he came up with his own confident analysis that there was no sound barrier. "The only barrier is bad aerodynamics and bad planning," he insisted. If Ridley said there was no sound barrier, then Yeager was not going to believe in one, even if some of the Air Force wags were privately dubbing the new round of test flights "Slick Goodlin's Revenge."

The X-1 flight program was a far cry from the instinctive, breakneck romps through the sky that Yeager so enjoyed. He was like a laboratory animal now, and his purpose was to provide data so that others could understand what was happening at high speeds. He was jabbed and poked and run through all manner of tests, most of which he hated. He especially dreaded the high-speed centrifuge that would spin him around like a top to acclimate him to the tremendous pressure of gravity in high-speed acceleration and turns.

While at Bell's Niagara Falls plant, Yeager was invited to

fire up the rocket engines in one of the Bell hangars. For the first time Yeager got an idea of just what kind of power he was dealing with. The engine shot out a huge arc of flame and burst forth with such a roar that Yeager had to cover his ears. When the entire building started shaking and plaster began to crack, Yeager was shaken to the core. What had he gotten himself into?

The flight procedure also demanded a harrowing bit of acrobatics far different from anything Yeager had experienced while flying an airplane. For reasons of both safety and efficiency, the X-1 did not take off under its own power. Takeoffs were the most dangerous stage of a flight, because if anything went wrong there was no room to maneuver. The X-1 would be carried high into the air under the belly of a Boeing B-29 bomber and then dropped. That way the pilot would have more time to correct whatever problems might arise. Although the X-1 was crammed with nearly 1,000 gallons of fuel, still that was barely enough to operate at full power for a few minutes. There was no point in wasting precious fuel on a takeoff.

Unfortunately, it was too dangerous to begin the flight with a pilot in the X-1 cockpit for fear that it might come loose from its cable. There was also no easy way for a pilot to get into the X-1 once it was off the ground. Yeager would have to climb down a ladder from the bomber into the X-1 in freezing temperatures while being pummeled by terrible winds. He declared that this descent into the cockpit was by far the most frightening part of any X-1 flight.

Before he could attempt to fly the X-1, Yeager had to first familiarize himself with the aircraft. Slick Goodlin did not make himself available to brief him on what he had learned during his 20 flights; so, Yeager had to discover everything for himself. The first flight was a glider trial without any fuel aboard. Once he made his first weak-kneed descent from the bomb bay of the B-29 Superfortress into the X-1, the rest was relatively easy.

Yeager was so pleased with the way the aircraft handled while gliding that he would not have minded taking a run at the sound barrier that very day. Anxious as the Air Force was to move ahead with the project, they found they had to rein in their daredevil pilot. Yeager was ordered to make three powerless flights to get comfortable with the handling before he was actually allowed to fly the X-1.

## FIRING THE ROCKETS

On August 29, 1947, Yeager was given permission to fire up the X-1 rocket chambers while in flight. His instructions were clear: he was to use only one of the craft's four rocket chambers at a time. A nice, easy ride would give him a chance to acclimate himself to the controls and monitors that governed each engine.

Yeager's instincts were put to the test the instant the plane was dropped from the bomber. The B-29 had been traveling slower than the X-1's minimum safe flying speed. As a result, when the X-1 was dropped, it stalled and fell, rear end first toward the ground. Yeager fought out of the stall, regained control, and reached for the ignition. Perhaps he recalled the power of the engine in that Niagara Falls hangar and knew that he was about to light a match to a bomb riding on the tail of his plane. In any case, as he moved the switch the rocket roared to life and Yeager experienced the characteristic X-1 mule kick that knocked him backward. Using only a quarter of its rocket power, the X-1 shot up in the sky at Mach .7.

For a veteran pilot like Yeager who had grown used to

the most outrageous thrills of air acrobatics, this was an entirely new experience, something like Mr. Toad at the wheel of his first motorcar. Yeager started doing things that neither Woolams nor Goodlin would ever have done. He reverted to the swashbuckling, country-boy behavior that had so often jeopardized his career. Instead of dumping his fuel and landing as his orders dictated, Yeager started playing. He performed a slow roll, forgetting that in the X-1 this maneuver could choke off the fuel supply and blow up the plane. Not content with that, he gave in to a sudden urge to show all those gloom-and-doom doubters that Chuck Yeager wasn't afraid of any sound barrier. He screamed down the runway only 300 feet off the ground, then opened up all four rocket chambers.

Slammed forward as if struck by a train, the X-1 shot straight up and blazed through the sky. A minute later the fuel ran dry, ending Yeager's joyride. By that time the X-1 was traveling Mach .85, Mach .3 faster than his orders allowed. All the shock-wave buffeting that Goodlin and the others had warned about appeared to be nothing more than a mirage. The X-1, the *Glamorous Glennis* (of course), was handling beautifully.

Although Yeager landed the plane safely, the NACA advisors wanted him thrown off the project. Colonel Boyd demanded a written explanation and apology for his behavior, and made it clear that the next time Yeager violated orders it would be his last flight in the X-1. This was one time that even Jack Ridley would not come to Yeager's defense. When Yeager asked for help in replying to Boyd, Ridley told him he was on his own.

That ended Yeager's hotdogging antics. From then on, he stuck closely to the flight plan. The programs' aeronautics experts recommended that they increase the speed of the X-1 by only Mach .02 per flight. Their wind-tunnel experiments so often broke down above Mach .85 that they had little data to go on in planning flights above that speed, so they wanted to proceed cautiously. Yeager and Ridley wanted to get on with it but dared not press their case. Yeager flew only twice a week in order to give the engineers a chance to digest the data from the previous flight.

Unlike the briefings that followed a Slick Goodlin flight, Yeager's reports were about as dramatic as reading a breakfast menu. (Goodlin had almost made his audience hear the rivets popping and feel the bone-jarring buffeting of the shock waves that battered his plane.) However, the Air Force was not as keen about publicity as Bell had been, so Yeager's reports were not given to outsiders. And even those cleared to listen to the tight-lipped pilot got little idea of what was happening to him as he rocketed toward the unknown territory above Mach .9. "Just the usual instability," he would shrug in his West Virginia drawl.

## YEAGER BUMPS THE SOUND BARRIER

On October 5, Yeager's sixth flight in the X-1, he finally experienced the power of the shock-wave forces that had torn apart so many airplanes and killed so many pilots. He was traveling at about Mach .86 when the aircraft began bouncing around as if it were racing over speed bumps in a parking lot. The right wing started to drop and it was all Yeager could do to hold it steady. He was not concerned about the heavy buffeting damaging the plane, for he knew how strong the X-1 was. But losing control over the airplane would be different.

The X-1 was wired from tip to tail with recording instruments, and the flight data from these instruments did not indicate that anything alarming was happening. But on the seventh powered flight, Yeager was streaking along at Mach .94 when he ran right up against what seemed to be a very solid sound barrier. The aircraft refused to respond to controls; Yeager could not get the plane to budge up or down.

It was the sort of situation that had previously cost many pilots their lives. Yeager, though, was fortunate enough to be making his trials in a spectacularly high-powered craft. Most other pilots who had been testing the limits of an airplane's speed had done so while in a power dive. When they had lost control, they were not in a position to recover. If the thicker, warmer air at low altitudes did not slow down the plane's Mach speed and allow them to regain control, the pilots continued straight into the ground. The X-1, on the other hand, was packed with ample power to go well beyond the sound barrier. Yeager could reach his desired speed while still traveling upward. All he had to do in this case was shut off the rockets, let gravity reduce his speed, and bring the plane back under control.

But now Yeager acknowledged the existence of a sound barrier. When he landed, he was convinced he had reached the end of the line in the X-1. There was no pilot alive who would risk trying for the speed of sound without being able to control the pitch of the plane. Colonel Boyd and the project advisors all glumly agreed that there was no point in going on.

There was still one man, though, who did not believe in the sound barrier. Jack Ridley puzzled over the problem, trying to figure out what sort of poor engineering was responsible for this latest setback. He finally concluded that the X-1 could retain just enough pitch control to get by if the pilot used an extra horizontal stabilizer system located on the tail. Maybe so, maybe not, thought the project advisors. That left it up to Yeager to decide if he wanted to risk it.

Yeager chose to go for it, but it was a far grimmer Chuck Yeager who stepped down the ladder into the cockpit than the one who had horsed around on that first X-1 flight. As he built up speed, he kept testing the stabilizer. It kept working, keeping his pitch level. At the critical Mach .94 he tried it again. Ridley was right. It was not perfect, but the stabilizer worked well enough that Yeager was willing to go ahead with further runs.

Just when he was breathing a sigh of relief over this, though, his windshield iced up. Yeager tried to claw it off with his fingernails, but it was built up too thick. Already drained from the pressure of the flight, Yeager had to land blind on Rogers Dry Lake, guided by directions from a chase pilot.

At that point most of the world knew little of what was happening at Muroc Army Air Field. Air Force and Bell Aircraft officials were still wary of challenging the mysterious sound barrier. But for Yeager and Ridley, the suspense was over. Once the elevator problem had been solved, the rest would be easy. There might be tremendous buffeting and some loss of control ("just the usual instability"), but nothing that posed any real concern to a pilot of Yeager's skill. He had already pushed the X-1 to Mach .955 (flight data would later show he had hit at least Mach .988 in testing the stabilizer); furthermore, Ridley and Yeager expected the shock-wave problems would diminish rather than increase as they passed the speed of sound. They were ready to agree with the late Jack Woolams—that the breaking of the sound barrier was going to be more like a laboratory experiment than a spectacular feat of courage. In fact, they could do it right now if they wanted to. Only, of course, the X-1 project directors still insisted on maintaining their cautious approach. The next flight, scheduled for Tuesday, October 14, would take the X-1 up to Mach .97. Yeager figured it would be another week or two before they inched their way up to the speed of sound.

## HORSING AROUND

The problem of pitch control had made for a stress-filled week, and Yeager needed to unwind on the weekend. Two days before the next flight, Chuck took Glennis out to Sunday dinner at the test pilots' favorite gathering spot, Pancho's Fly Inn. Besides serving food and providing pilot camaraderie, Pancho's also had a riding stable. As Glennis had always been fond of horses and was an excellent rider, Chuck suggested the two of them go for a moonlit ride in the desert.

The brisk ride quickly turned into a hotly contested race. Daring Glennis to beat him back to Pancho's corral, Chuck shot off into the lead. Once again he had reverted to the wild, fun-seeking, risk-taking Chuck Yeager. The driving rhythm of the galloping horses may have lulled Chuck into forgetting that he was a test pilot, conducting the most important flight experiments since the Wright brothers.

This time Yeager's legendary eyesight missed something; he failed to see that someone had shut the corral while they were out. His horse hit the gate, and Chuck went flying so hard he nearly knocked himself out. As he stood up groggily, the pain in his right side nearly doubled him over. Clutching a couple of broken ribs, he was in such pain that Glennis wanted to get him to the base doctors.

Instantly Yeager realized he had stepped over the line once too often. No Army doctor would let a pilot fly the X-1 with two broken ribs. Tuesday's run would be postponed; maybe even another pilot would be found to take over. Neither possibility was acceptable to Yeager. So, he secretly visited a physician in the nearby small town of Rosemond who taped him up.

Worried that he might not be able to fly, Yeager slept poorly on Monday night. Although his arm was almost useless, he found that he could drive an automobile and hoped that operating the controls of the aircraft would be no more physically taxing. But how was he going to push the handle that locked the X-1 door once he was inside? The cockpit was so small that he could not turn and use his left arm, and a few quick tests convinced Yeager that he could never shut the door with his right arm. The flight would have to be cancelled. It might seem a small problem, but it was going to bump him out of a place in history.

Before giving up, Yeager turned to Jack Ridley for help. As usual, Ridley came up with a clever solution. He asked a custodian to cut off about nine inches of a broom handle. Using that as a lever, Yeager might be able to get the door shut.

Nothing that happened at Pancho's ever remained a secret for long among the pilots at Muroc. As Yeager strolled into the hangar before his ninth powered X-1 flight, he was presented a carrot, a pair of glasses, and a rope in memory of his unfortunate "bronco" ride. But no one breathed a word to his supervisors, and Yeager prepared for the flight.

The X-1 trials were run under the Army's usual umbrella of secrecy. Only a handful of essential workers were on the scene as the B-29 "mother-plane" prepared to take off. Yeager entered the silver bomber and sat down on a metal box to wait.

The bomber, piloted by Bob Cardenas, took off. It rose into the air in a spiral to make sure that the X-1 was launched above the dry lake landing bed. Quietly, Yeager and Ridley waited until the heavy, lumbering plane reached 5,000 feet.

"Let's go," Yeager said.

No matter how many times he had done it, Yeager still found the trip down the ladder terrifying. Trying to get down those steel steps with the freezing wind battering him was bad enough when he was healthy. The pain in his side made it torture.

Yeager managed to reach the orange and white X-1 and stepped gingerly into it. He could never get over the feeling that the cable holding the plane to the B-29 would snap as soon as he put his weight onto it.

Three pieces of equipment waited for him inside the cramped X-1 cockpit. There was a helmet, a World War II tank driver's model that Yeager had adapted to protect his head from smacking the cockpit walls during the hard buffeting. There was an oxygen mask, so that he could breathe inside his nitrogen-filled cockpit. And there was the broom handle. Yeager inserted it into the latch, and with some effort, got the door shut.

## "MAKE A NOTE, RIDLEY"

He was sitting in the darkness, scrunched down with his knees higher than his shoulders. It was cold in the cockpit refrigerated by supercooled liquid oxygen. This was the other part of the ride that Yeager most dreaded: the drop.

When B-29 pilot Cardenas reached 20,000 feet, he leveled off and asked Yeager if he was ready. At Yeager's okay, the B-29 went into a dive to pick up speed so that the X-1 would not stall out upon launching. Yeager heard that resounding crack of the cables as they released. As the X-1 dropped into the sky, "my heart was in my mouth and my stomach right behind it." Despite the dive, the B-29 was still flying too slowly. The X-1 began to stall.

Squinting from the sudden brightness after being holed up in the B-29 belly, Yeager assumed control. Wasting no time, he fired all four rockets, one after another, and raced away from the two "chase" planes that were assigned to check on his safety. Yeager had been told to hold it below Mach .96 unless he was sure the plane could handle more. At about Mach .88 the shock waves began battering the plane. Yeager fought through it, made good use of his stabilizers, and shut off two of the rockets. The X-1 continued to pick up speed as it climbed to nearly eight miles above the earth.

At that point Yeager leveled off and refired the third rocket engine. The X-1 shot ahead and reached Mach .95, then Mach .96. Yeager sensed that the shock waves were diminishing the faster he went. There was no reason to pull back. So Yeager did nothing. He just let the X-1 do what it was designed to do.

The Machmeter moved up to .965, then suddenly jumped. Yeager thought there was something wrong with his vision. The needle went off the scale and stayed there for 18 seconds, while Yeager enjoyed the smoothest ride of his life. He had sailed beyond the sound barrier!

In the years that followed, Yeager was asked countless times to recall exactly what happened in the next few seconds. The question began to frustrate him. "I've tried to think back on that first flight past Mach 1, but it doesn't seem any more important than the other (flights)," he reminisced. "It was just a matter of flying the airplane. I was kind of disappointed it wasn't more of a big charge than it was."

"Just a matter of flying the airplane." "Just the usual instability." That was Chuck Yeager. But then when Wilbur and Orville Wright had first flown at Kitty Hawk, they had been unemotional, too. Perhaps it was because they had simply accomplished the goal they knew was within their reach. For Yeager, too, it was just "flying the airplane." Never mind that he was doing the job with two broken ribs, a fact that never seems to come up in any of his accounts of the actual flight.

Even though he was just flying an airplane, Yeager had to let Jack Ridley know that he had been right about everything. Ridley, back in the B-29, had been conversing with Yeager throughout the flight, and Yeager could easily have told him what happened. But the Air Force insisted on keeping this all top secret, and not even Yeager was going to be accused of spilling military secrets over the airwaves. Still it was only fair that Ridley be the first to know what was going on.

"Hey Ridley! Make another note," Yeager said, calmly. "There's something wrong with this Machmeter. It's gone completely screwy!"

The words might have sounded innocent enough to anyone listening in on their frequency. But Ridley knew very well what Yeager was saying.

Forty miles away from Muroc Army Air Field, in Victorville, California, there was another clue as to what had happened eight miles high above the desert. For the first time in history, humans heard the sonic boom of a rocket plane exceeding the speed of sound.

Had Yeager's exploits been plastered on the front page of the newspapers the next day, he would have been the most exalted aviator since the Wright brothers. But the Air Force was determined to keep its test data secret. Even when *Aviation* magazine snooped out the story and published a brief report of the historic flight two months later, the Air Force refused to confirm it. Not until June of 1948 was the truth finally acknowledged. By then Yeager had flown dozens of flights in the X-1, including one in which he took off without the assist of the B-29, and flew to a speed of Mach 1.45. By that time, surpassing the speed of sound had almost become routine.

The sound barrier had dissolved as mysteriously as it had appeared. Jack Ridley had said there was no impenetrable wall in the sky; Chuck Yeager had gone ahead and proved it on October 14, 1947.

Yet the sound barrier was no mirage. It may not have been exactly what people expected it to be, but it was real. The benefit of hindsight shows us that the sound barrier was not so much a wall as a minefield of hidden dangers all detonated by the powerful effects of shock waves. That field had to be cleared before Chuck Yeager could make his daring flight and outrun the speed of sound. In that respect, Yeager alone did not break the sound barrier. It was broken by many pilots, some known and some who remain nameless, many of whom sacrificed their lives, by engineers, designers, and aircraft manufacturers. All of them helped break through the invisible barrier to supersonic flight and so ushered the twentieth century into the space age.

# Glossary

*biplane*  an airplane with two sets of wings

*buffeting*  irregular shaking and bouncing due to turbulent air flow

*compressibility*  the disturbance of air flow caused by the compression of air that occurs in front of an object moving at very high speeds

*dive brakes*  flaps that can be adjusted to slow down an airplane during a dive

*drag*  the aerodynamic force that works against the airplane's forward motion

*elevator*  a movable piece attached to the tail of the airplane by which a pilot can control the vertical (up-and-down) movement of the plane

*flying wing*  an airplane in which the center of the plane is not much thicker than the wings

*gas turbine*  a rotary engine whose blades are turned by hot gas under intense pressure from compressed air

*jet*  an airplane powered by an engine such as the gas turbine that produces a forward movement by the steady powerful flow of pressurized gases shot toward the rear of the plane

*lift*   the upward force produced by airflow over the wings that opposes the force of gravity

*Mach number*   a number corresponding to the percentage of the speed of sound, taking into account air temperature as well as airplane speed; Mach $1.0 =$ the speed of sound

*monoplane*   an airplane with one set of wings

*photographic timing*   a method of timing in which photographs are taken at precise intervals and the distance covered between photographs is measured

*power dive*   a maneuver in which a pilot accelerates an airplane directly toward the ground

*rocket engine*   an engine powered by the discharge of gases created from the reaction of burning liquid or solid fuel

*rotary engine*   engine developed by Louis and Laurent Seguin in which the entire body of the engine spun along with the propellers

*rudder*   a movable piece attached to the tail of the plane that controls horizontal (side-to-side) direction

*shock waves*   a wave of compression formed around an object whenever that object exceeds the speed of sound

*sound barrier*   term given to the effects of compressibility that became so severe as an airplane approached the speed of sound that it presented a barrier to increased airplane speed

*swept wing*   a wing that angles back toward the tail of the plane instead of projecting straight out from the fuselage

*V-1 "buzz bombs"*   a type of German long-range missile fired at England during World War II

# Further Reading

Angelucci, Enzo. *Airplanes: From the Dawn of Flight to the Present Day.* New York: McGraw-Hill Book Company, 1973.

Boyne, Walter J. *The Smithsonian Book of Flight for Young People.* New York: Atheneum, 1988.

Bryan, C. D. B. *The National Air and Space Museum.* New York: Harry N. Abrams, 1979.

Courtlandt, Canby. *A History of Flight.* New York: Hawthorn, 1963.

Crossfield, A. Scott. *Always Another Dawn: The Story of a Rocket Test Pilot.* Cleveland: The World Publishing Company, 1960.

Green, William. *Rocket Fighter.* New York: Ballantine, 1971.

Hallion, Richard P. *Supersonic Flight: Breaking the Sound Barrier and Beyond; The Story of the Bell X-1 and Douglas D-558.* New York: Macmillan, 1972.

Josephy, Alvin M., Jr., ed. *The American Heritage History of Flight.* New York: American Heritage Publishing Co., Inc., 1962.

Lomax, Judy. *Women of the Air.* New York: Dodd Mead, 1987.

Sweetman, Bill. *High Speed Flight.* London, UK: Jane's, 1983.

Taylor, John W. *History of Aviation.* New York: Crown, 1972.

Thomas, Shirley. *Men of Space.* Vol. 1. Philadelphia: Chilton, 1960.

Time-Life Books. *Designers and Test Pilots*. Alexandria, VA.: Time-Life Books, 1983.

Time-Life Books. *Flight*. Alexandria, VA.: Time-Life Books, 1990.

Von Braun, Wernher. *History of Rocketry and Space*. New York: Crowell, 1975.

Wolfe, Tom. *The Right Stuff*. New York: Farrar, Straus & Giroux, 1979.

Wragg, David W. *Speed in the Air*. New York: Frederick Fell, 1974.

Yeager, Chuck and Leo Janos. *Yeager: an Autobiography*. New York: Bantam, 1985.

# Index

# About the Author

Nathan Aaseng has published more than 90 books for young readers on a wide variety of subjects. He majored in both English and Biology at Luther College (Iowa) and worked as a microbiologist prior to taking up full-time writing in 1979. His books have been included on recommended lists of the Child Study Association of America and of Children's Book Council joint committees with the National Science Teachers Association, the National Council for the Social Studies, and the International Reading Association. He lives in Eau Claire, Wisconsin, with his wife and four children.